ILIASSA SEQUIN

COLLECTED COMPLETE POEMS

T0352367

Iliassa Sequin

Collected Complete Poems

*Edited by Anthony Howell from manuscripts
supplied by Ken Sequin*

Grey Suit Editions

First published in 2021 by
Grey Suit Editions, an affiliate
of Phoenix Publishing House Ltd
Reprinted in 2021, 2023

British Library Cataloguing in Publication Data
A C.I.P. catalogue record for this book is available
from the British Library

Paperback ISBN: 978-1-903006-23-8
e-book ISBN: 978-1-903006-24-5

Designed and typeset by Anvil

Printed and bound in the United Kingdom
by Hobbs the Printers Ltd

The photograph of Iliassa Sequin is by Katarina Carlquist

Grey Suit Editions
33 Holcombe Road, London N17 9AS
https://greysuiteditions.co.uk/

A note on this edition

ILIASSA SEQUIN was in the habit of constantly altering and adjusting her poetic output. There are variants to every line she wrote. Drafts abound of every poem in this collection, and there are also unfinished pieces and collaborations. The work of this poet resembles the tapestry that Penelope insisted that she had to complete before accepting the hand of any of her suitors, the tapestry that she wove in the day and undid every night. Thus the job of the editor is of necessity a creative one. It resembles the act of interpretation that is epitomized by the notion of a 'version'. The issue is that of sensibility, rather than of accuracy.

This is partly because of the difficulty of establishing which is the 'final' version of any particular poem, but it is also because of the poet's unique style. Iliassa Sequin often relinquished capital letters – feeling that there was a lack of democracy expressed through giving certain letters special status. When she does capitalise, one senses a specific purpose, an emphasis. Musicality is of more urgency than clarity of meaning. Words are spilt like musical notes in an expressive modernist score, or created on the white 'Mallarméan' page as if that page were a canvas. Her quintets repeat phrases and work in sequence, as might a series of paintings. The suggestive results are to be perceived through the subjective interpretation of the reader – there may be no concise and specific meaning. Readers seem invited to make the meaning in their mind, as with many an abstract painting. There is a deliberate ambivalence, and suggestive phrases elide as in a line from 'the unfinished painting': 'I created a fuss of all kinds of weapons – drugs and sex' – for here the 'fuss of' gives a hint of 'I made a mess of', so one understands why the 'of' is not 'about'. The poet also uses apostrophes as a form of punctuation, creating a slight hesitation before and after a phrase – but with a purpose that is not as grammatical as a comma. It is more a matter of making that phrase distinct, highlighted, as a passage in a painting might be.

I have worked from manuscripts supplied by her husband, and tried to present a collection of poems which appear to have a 'complete' version. However, one could haggle for a thousand years over the finality of any line and its accuracy. Rather than allow Iliassa Sequin's poems to languish in the throes of unresolvable debate, Grey Suit Editions has chosen to present an initial version of her poems. A second volume, comprising variant readings, collaborations, drafts and unfinished projects could certainly be published in the future.

Finally I should like to acknowledge Peter Jay's invaluable contribution to the editing of these poems, together with that of the poet's husband, Ken Sequin.

ANTHONY HOWELL, 2020

Contents

quintets 1–5   11

routechart   29

    14 quartets & 19 quintets

cyprian quartets   97

    12 quartets

modern Greece   125

    4 quintets

two cinema sextets   141

the rights of sanctuary   153

    4 Aristophanian quintets

words on poetry   165

kursk – 69°40′N 37°35′E   169

    15 quintets & 2 quartets

le tableau inachevé   217

gas black   227

    4 quintets

love fragments   239

    11 quintets

richard dadd   267

    septet

prosodion   273

    the dolphins of arion

    a dissembled love song

    prosodion

    the muse thalia's abodes

Brief Biography   289

Notes and Acknowledgements   293

quintets 1–5

quintet 1

I

i wish of boredom
an oath on never
oh! I was spoken to thus oh! thus
        'gaily love'

with gluttonous tears
        'urging for the forgiving margins'

        behind a gaze of sorrow
        'nibbling at relish'
        oh! I am enchanted, a captive

II

pleasure
intended in morninghood to last
with fear

as a child
startled, beset on assuaged barrenness
of fetish undergrounds

– through unmoved bypaths, slightly rescued

diminished fantasies   'allured me'

III

self-conquered joy
dear, dear, she, converting her bias
wasteful, by a compass – due
                              oppressed

living, she no longer shares
     'who glides away with it
     who compels the fees'

of scattered hours, deficient
                              in heavens

IV

hasten to blur foolish heart

in prettiest water's pursuits
be drowned

                    'recalled by a demure feast
                    of chained safeguards
                    or unconfined

aloof worshipped from sea-agate carcasses'

V

would you confound – in dual languor
another artifice of sapped inventions, interred smiles

       as if the moon miscarried
       her inanimate yellow

elsewhere disburdened from below the desert
a coward trophy

quintet 2

I

callous and faultless, he smote upwards the hooks
in their disproportion

>   in the mincing rounds, as a prize-fighter
>   emaciated with fattened, caressing
>   fisticuffs
>   discharging
>
>   beneath succulent strangers

II

conjured by green, destitute yellow
our superstitions shifted from jealousy

unfaithfully rambling in 'chaste' parodies
of 'savage' intercourses
with travestied errors
on 'venial' red

white persecutions solaced . . .

III

what have you subverted, enticingly
                              'cradled with knives'

mollusc-wrought lips, perhaps to ruminate
on the embowelled meal's sagacity

                    unevenly – rapturous in libertine partitions
'sanctioned between beheaded elegies'

IV

as petty-playing hope succumbed, emboldened centaurs
tempted

                    a moorish sojourn
                    in the ripened autumn
                    'unsaddled tales' elgarian reprisals

as a child usurped by fabled tears

V

elusory with a verse's compass, in fretful mockery
she chose

        – rowing inflections
        aslant, towards carrion syllables' waning
        echoes

hardened from tender intermissions' decrying
silence

quintet 3

I

invoked
unattempted?
having compiled 'injuries' anew
remiss, an unaware loss

ah! what has mattered, has silence
indicted Narcissus, dimpled with solace

                                    unhappiest, wilful

dear ends
edged in sleety tenderness

II

being curbed in your resemblance – to its sluggish bounds
    in the cloistral huddle

time forestalls

    'an unfinished sneer's distraught laughter
    in unfulfilled redemption – from our waney likeness'

III

whereas sealed, craven-bare sameness in me
was transgressed by you

      'again we lied'

      of a premonition (at an old recess)
      throughout forerunning the youth of orchids'
      slightest ashes, each unsheltered

IV

how many hours 'altercations' interred fears . . .

how many infrangible numbers of a vanishing axis
slowly betokened

      almost surmised
      from a forbidden negligence
      how many acceded

V

slowly turning from retrograde passions
the passengers – on infantine carcasses – surrendered

'scourged by dreams of an iambic rescue'

on their second shrouded tideless voyage
in circumcised memories

quintet 4

I

adhering to melancholy
perhaps she rivals in mute fables deafened nightingales
'the shriek-beaten echoes of an unyielding voice'

perhaps ensnared in
dissuasive contests – she slackened the umbrage
to her ear

II

waterlilies' sun-slaughtered blossoms, dislodged from
swooning leaves

> on the sulfurous boundary
> sleighs of shades-in-twilight-ashes
> encountered with my heart's nativity of shadows

III

being brought against white buoyant intercourses
                                    and turbid moisture

i submitted in water, under the glutinous verge
distilled from your conspiracy
   through the jelly of hatred

                                    in iridescence

IV

should I defer
the evening's lisp
                  until infused in brazen retention
                  the auburn features of entrenchment
                  aged,
            players with quarried toys
            lovers who have impaired th'utterance o'flesh
                  distempered

V

taught in yellow clay of crusty skills
(performed by her fathers)

how to bribe

>with a sharper past's bruised inheritance, abroad
>superfluous, willingly-caressing satyrs' secrets

aspersed for moanful nakedness

quintet 5

I

self-mutilated traitors
without hands 'dismembered from caresses'

in oarless massacres of sunken prints, they were drawn
by knives' surveyors

                              stealthily daubing – slitting
under an unravelling wrist, toward its compassion

II

below uneven heights, woeful fertility dissolved in
                                                similitudes

                    amber primroses' boisterous prime
                    still wet
                    against daunting lovers

being furrowed in dissipated laxity
          . . . being compared

III

under its bridal spears, the morning's groom has buried
                                        the lugging sun

            'huddled in placid drowsiness
            vengeful for slumberous echoes'
            steering through streamlets of dance

IV

endowed with – her vaulted lips of a brief price
                        contiguous mirrors breaking down

the night's image barters their travesty
            'its deficit of saturation in his assaulted body
            for her buyer's artificial wounds'

V

enclosed aloof with unbidden jesters' nibbling colours
'tumble and skating laughter'

        inherent green,
        divisible red imitations of which they lied
                    of either's sanctity
                  in darkness

immured with him

routechart

14 quartets & 19 quintets

1 quintet

I

poor dreamer
heedless of a forward sight aligned up to the rear
unquestioningly warding off a blind alley of words
barring their unfathomed solitude

II

dear, dear
self-imagined joy
din on the dot a sorrow
she no longer strikes up
dear, dear she
her dumb show
ran to waste
her impromptu heaven
sick at heart
held terror

III

chaos swamped putrefied athens
invulnerable through gangling lips
inwrought with the hazards of democracy
she, under unicorn as monstrous as heavenly

IV

wildandwhirling words have been at fault
(improbable as a silent contraction of the tenor
defiant in its endeavour to weep
unrelentingly in awe of the untempered)

V

written in the margin, stroke by grecian stroke
sodomy over carrion's pittance

insidiously lit unpalatable noun-clusters lay unreserved
concurrent with the slaughter of democracy

2 quartet

I

whereas i am i am also a no ball

again bowling over the wicket
dreams hasten past

whereas i am
i am also inconsolably boundless

again a greenish reflex hugged the wind
defying 'face to face' ribaldry

again a haunted maiden over
wards off
their latent ritual

II

to the scale of one melancholic city
(solicitous for its dwelling
inebriated on grief) i live

not an expiatory tear has been rendered
neither a breath nor a voice yield account
nowhere the barriers were removed

III

patience overreached time
(it happened upon a distraught sneer's remodelled
laughter
at unfulfilled redemption from terra incognita –
   once again? why, yes, driven forward
to urge the storm clouds)

IV

thereby hangs a tale . . .
bereft of a rose, no shelter is given

blossom per blossom – time remits the signal defeat
unduly . . . endlessly on exhaling its familiar sermon

3 quartet

I

sired by the poet pindar
pegasus will run its life's riot
it will dream of an ever widening gap

onwards violet-wreathed utopias . . .

lingering on impish reflections
it will swear treason against the stud

beaten at a frantic gallop
kissing the syracusan turf within striking distance

heedful of his own death

II

irish bloodstock

fair thyona in foal roused
– under harsh-voiced lullabies . . .
barbarously callous to the silent transmission of pleading
                                        excellence

(. . . racing dear against a solitary life? . . .)

III

foot race

dog-tired dreams . . . erring on shadows' untrodden edges
how they dither
crowned at olympian xii
how derisively wandering in memory's incongruous split

IV

nothing is ebbing out
sibilant omens on all their journeys
violet eerie whistling aberrations of the autumn
 . . . thawing leaves . . . innate loneliness in their path

4 quartet

I

he swung his foot towards the bloated goal
taunt for taunt in pursuit
embracing the air

motionlessly
love is perpetually nonchalant

angled in the vista of a fleeing recollection
as in 'where and why'
it never touched the rebounded ball

nor amiss the brazilian winger

II

man utd – made in the image of god

growing up in a frenzy – their childhood recovered its goal
in so brittle a fight huddled together in music

he himself in fair rebellion, impatience-struck

III

what a fool, under the cover of a fancy throw-in
ball-stalking   dribbling . . .
the stag simulates the ball
each runs out ahead . . . either has fallen together

IV

the night was purchased in the fullness of love –
in the undercurrent of the underdog
– flesh would be misgiven –
she, as if for nothing inured to invisible mirrors

5 quintet

I

greek chart

wrangling with incessant seafogs
white spongy grounds of ancient water
slid noiselessly by her
edgewise . . . a weightless mud has been drawn blueclear
reaching luminous range

II

V of S

roundabout, dislodged, impartial to her abduction

(neither her mutilated arms resting on the beams of victory
nor awakened in the harvest home

bid her farewell)

her charted wings hauled taut to the sky

III

why ingest mollusc-wrought lips 'clusters of desire'
perhaps in hunger – deliberating on unbounded sex

the sap of youth a mere similitude
licentiously tendered on a plate of wisdom
          O glutton, salome

IV

more wanton effigies they have summoned up
begging to dream from hand to mouth
more endearing self possessions, more equal deaths
from an extraneous barrenness to a mock reflection

V

(the iambic ship remained stationary
assuming to the contrary a surge athwart fair iona
impervious to ulysses' arrival

wallowing caressing the green ferment of the sea)

6 quartet

I

on the moonless watch
de la terre à la lune
on a mock wave crest

flown in the contrary orbit . . .

between split mountains . . .
towards the evening star . . .
misquoting a phallic ceremony

twenty thousand leagues under the sea
slumberous I awoke

II

ventriloquial

rattled at childhood
the mouth hears its shouting
lips belie the clamour

in defiance of any unwon memory
annihilating any languid shelter?

III

beneath outofjoint masks, a smile stiffens . . .
conjured up over twirling scourges of a wit . . .
stretched out of a dual reversal of the whole face
razored by the intermedium of death

IV

engaging in a boorish semblance of patricide
titania sleeping
seized upon sweetened shadows
cast in fairylike intimations . . .
encountered on her literal surrender . . .
fraught with fraudulent red
by richard dadd

7 quartet

I

within striking distance
from the painted lady
nothing seems so far away

segmental, shimmering
rabid tortuous
without wings

having redrawn
the limbless funfair
o'er legsheadantennae
blue hallowed thorax

II

you may discount our friendship
without words

or forswear its rise and fall
on verbal subtleties

if only perhaps unbeknown of the older child's betrayal
  – love was never intended

III

being tortured on the bias towards instantaneous joy
as if by default on penalty of retreating
    sensually balled off limits
in thespian disguise   (as if i care a heavenly damn)

IV

who snatched the umbilical cord
from below the curve of his thigh

unavoidably offensive, whose scathing passion
    reaps the grotesque of maturity . . .

8 quintet

I

cherry burton pond

assuaged in the throes of repellent melancholy

a swan, its ethereal dalliance incessantly
losing to motionless adolescents
slid by fatal pleasures

II

querulously motherless, have we concurred to wait
in kindred rancour on the bolster of fear

(imbued with her mopish kisses' torrent
until the air enshrouds her breath, swaying twice)

III

either he sprinkled his drunken benediction
or she avowed herself the imitative eunuch

as a reproof to her male demented death
when he spilt his infantile glass over her

IV

the faltering dancer

rapturous bodies, muscle-bound ceased to dance
                    indulgently infirm, deliciously unremitting
swerving tortuously under bloodshot performers
                    chartered to the lydian mode

V

have we been acquitted of indecency
enacted in our hermaphrodite wanton prison

in no doubt about the amorous offensive
railed at the shrine of either's otherness

9 quintet

I

the rhetoric of war

how often
grovelling tongues due to rejoicing
solstitial excuses
were absolved

hawklike mouthed
hinged on slippery trophies

II

how often
words connived at skirmished defeats . . .

recalcitrant lipped
with an eloquent forgery's bad break
(negotiable for a short eternity)

III

it was as the only child of an effete juggler
        stipulated for amusement
with the avarice of stringent crimson
impressed on her suckling's face
            – perhaps to interface with the encrusted plot

IV

under compulsion, beaten hollow against a shower of
                                        pleasures
        swear 'off drink'

entrusted by the merry dionysian to revel in thirst
        befogged in an emerald-bout of dreams
'unmistakably alone am i'

V

        veering towards his martian squadrons
he a parodist cocked the weapon

        flying by languid venus
melodiously self-propelled in the ennui of a wanton
                                        schoolboy

10   quintet

I

for Paul Celan

a charred rose was inserted in between the niemandrose
as with one exclamation of terror
crumbling without fragrance or colour
except in the vowel of the pronoun I

II
why is fire exempted from ashes, reduced to
                                        incomprehension

singed children
under unfolding layers of lives forestalled
deciphered in mournful verse by you alone

III

he put the question 'how and why'
to oscillate between one unnamable utterance of spleen

or whether to borrow towards its ashen denial
in search of the intermediary poem's furnace

IV

whether the niemandrose bears witness to a winter flower
open, in silent blossom

or whether it has disbudded the riot of language
nevertheless, glowing amok, in it i read myself

V

in vertical detours, the green hunches of waves
captured dolphins almost (benumbed)

unpityingly resonant through swirling vowels
which (retracted) their ulcerous melody

II quintet

I

preempting the chapter on springtime
may i read to you of its harbinger
 'one impatient swallow – a cutting grey, scissorwinged
subsiding into its own incongruous numbness
  foraged for a last breath
anticipating anew the right to violence'

II

stroke by eddying stroke
a fool's butterfly loiters aslant

unaccountably for, as if it were playing cupid,
fallen in all haste 'gathered to itself'
  immobile even in dance

III

how many distended flowers the air kissed
how many indigo butterflies
'stooping to conquer' rejoiced in love
how much a child's innocence is taken as a disadvantage

IV

in memory of titania

the autumn devours itself

swooping from leaf to leaf
in want of flowers
its appetite arose

each petal's youthful carrion
compensating for the other
has fallen in love

V

baulked at death's revolution
one bower of roses
enflamed in dance
quivers

in pursuit of ragged titania . . .
sulphureous colours joined in

12 quartet

I

roving over sunk island
emaciated seagulls
are sucked inshore

wallowing at random
their wings, semen of the famished sky
to be dispensed from my mouth

II

to RLS

let go the illicit margins
in the utter air of rebellion in the horny gutters
of the freighter's berth unloading his mercurial visions
(I hauled over an open book)

III

eager to scare
        obstinate lenders are rolling back
flirtatious expansions of jaundiced currency
        strewn on lacerated images
piously held in my fingers' rowlock

IV

sports news

by the code of love
the ball in play is disputed
by each aggressor's alternating fault

on the Grecian baseline (Wimbledon's *trompe l'œil*)
unctuous strawberries underexposed
are bestrewed on craven shadows
– slimy expectations being on offer –
in the deuced court as a receiver having succumbed
to the next ancient point

advantage nausicaa

13 quintet

I

the affected riot stumbles . . .
elusive singers
echoing drunken leers
tickling the fancy
of girlie urchins
were gnawn into a morass

II

disheartened children
conspicuous dwarfs
slyly entrapped in rickety embraces
bustling about – under a cloud –
on the streets by stealth
– tripping up their melancholy

III

the spinner trundles down the wicket –
sweeping up claywefts of morning-dust

– set at variance – as in a haphazard masquerade
forcibly bowling against the pivot of superseding shadows

IV

fate has been returned tenfold
negotiably tender slippery hopes
fire-eaters' money – jugglers
reckoned with decrepit hands
rotating 'the lucky fool'
under the heels of frosty fire

V

on a yorkshire terrier

in the time that still remains to bubble over
and as yet on account of being dispatched
forsaken vigils were drawn from memory
meanwhile fair-seeming with my brutish old cock

14 quintet

I

Truinas A de B

when doting giants
from the swooping core of their roots
sway in truant heights
bearing witness to tremulous blossoms
for spring's forbidden shrinkage
on time's curved accuracy, will i remember . . .

II

oh dear, so intolerably aroused
         I will hesitate no more

in falsifying death, emulous of conceited wounds
         written across her razored wrist

III

the rose sediment was congealed
– it gathers fulfilment
pleasure's indebted mouth, its withdrawal from a sour
                                        residue
in tranquillity, enunciating the words of a loved one

IV

while the blubber boils
he being sold on
at the rate of a whale caught blind
charged with illiquid stinginess . . .
barbarous to its dissolution . . .
unforgivingly reaping the scum of the relics

V

remember 'the controversial passage of modern Iphigeneia'

below paternal groins the sky opened the sea bled
slid to the point of no return

remember 'how far from here she resounds
off the trading weather'

(for O.E.)

15 quintet

I

low mass

have you surrendered the shrine of the golden deer
was its carrion so pure

converged towards the black island's anger
weaving into lighter warps among the dying

II

percussive voices stutter mutinous deirdre's blood overture –

    deaf-mute drum majorettes
fractured in silence with hollow shrieks
    urging a tongueless singer to comply   over and out

III

anew detained for the murders of his suckling
I bid farewell to the fair irish
bleeding to a fault . . .
cradled in dogged carrion among the shrouds of trojan
                      Ulster

IV

raising the siege of St Patrick
he envisaged star-like prayers

conniving at the trumpery of war
scattering evil through the air

sanctimoniously gun-purging

V

a sluggish rose abiding by the prurience of enmity
withers
elusory combatants rivalling the palest shamrock
unvindicated by the tremor of imbroglio arose

16 quartet

I

rocked by the silent shifts
of night . . .
one aqueous note
swooping upon
fourteen disruptive colours

minus five discordant sounds
pleading rebellion

the stringent third
redlunarviolet
in the voluptuous sixth
honed on music

hammers out the alluring bass

II

for its indemnity at supper, on a charge of drunkenness

the audience of gummy Irish, in pain, coaxed another
interchangeably deluxe vagary
                'kick against the pricks'
obsequious english by default, weeping and laughing away

III

submissive to its errors in the fragmentary clouds
piercing its rival on his wounded pirouette

spilling its blood the night shortens
pricking with derision at our next encounter

IV

deprived of vigour, a minor key ceased
(anew as of a youthful ox under the brewing age of
                                        consent . . .
embedding its melancholic groans unto bucolics)

as it were, mellifluous shrills bludgeon the pastoral poem

17 quartet

I

illicit shadows foraged in grey circuits
swarmed over trafficking –
post-Ford Dagenham contrived to reproach
the mule-car race –

composts of wheels being entangled
incest and treason were preordained

saucily undertaken to rebuke
blithering Dagenham emulating funeral Thebes

II

rugby league . . .

barrel-chested with obsequious feet, expostulatory hands
   treacherously 'knocked on'
in the first unholy instance of the lion's mouth

   in due combat aligned he might 'win the day'
guilt-free elbowed into intemperance

III

– a try was converted, in default of the runners-up
it put forth its barren image
threatened with rousing desire for its pestilent residue
having no other misnomer for his goal average

IV

a witness of minimum age with punitive affection decried
        nothing, having vouched for fair cruelty
where and when only too slyly
        Punch seized Judy

18 quartet

I

blithering tongues imbued with derision
dire, bitter, swollen an' drunken bitten
        shoved off thirst

treacherously sweet acid lips
under compulsion
swarming in a tour de force, hung over

sprinkled on the roots of eerie drunkenness . . .

engulfing the kinks of a falstaffian mouth
        their dionysian course unaltered

it was a clear-cut wound
chiselled to the colours of love

shorn through incipient yellow

it might re-fester sub-delirious red
        of undertinted rot

bevelled to pitch-darkness

II

standpoint 'leprinceauxfleursdelis'

conspicuously bewildered in Cretan attire . . .
undimmed redblackyellow petals
forgathered under an illusion of carnival
abetting youth's wildest summer

III

who needs to remember an old face
            inscrutable in its diversion

after the last sunrise of the spring
            the summer's shaken complicity

disputing the autumn of cyprian venus?

IV

venus de milo

picking over her aphrodisiac torso
would he be disburdened of the gracious fissures
plunder or ravishment

as if to bear witness to its own mutilation
cut across askew for the passage of decay

19 quartet

I

st caravaggio the inexpiable sinner

poverty stricken
thread-bare
salome
extruded from heavenly wreckage

hips, groins, belly and thigh
the red hair dissolved at sunrise

unequivocally in default of parsimonious feelings
exhaling the slaughtered breath
of time, unresentful

II

a kiss being escorted to its burial of love

he as her, how much are we concealing
she more than him, salome's glacial acid
rationed to the edge of registered bodies
hers, self-incised 'a new waxen image'
remains

III

had not the bridegroom been as fair
bowed in self-communion

at the age of puberty
from a disruptive childhood
under his thighbone's virgin blood

enduring corporal punishment on his thawing body . . .

IV

whose reflux of tears ever so cannily
occur in stagnant water

what would it matter to the beast in narcissus *to rise*
to the bait
focused on limpid mirrors
as if bent to the shadows of tremulous forms

20 quartet

I

poultry

you'll augur well for a cock's infirmity
  it may be that you were
        his limestonecarrion-child shaken from electrons
perhaps I its staunch executioner

II

blinkered – she keeps vigil

foolishly subjugated by a dogged death
– hesitant over incurable wounds

as if one consensual parody of happiness
was abandoned
as if it was her outgoing hope
off base grounded

III

bustling about at full passion –
I rode my mule at dulcinea's length

inexhaustibly contriving to milk the idle ram

further in mire milled by verse
caught in the tendon
of the least invulnerable

IV

'spare the rod and spoil the odds' . . .

      as a trumpet flower's horse-like image
roused the tender maiden

ridden askance . . . transfixed in pastoral relapses

      wittingly chivalrous . . .
as the 2,000 guineas residue remains over

21 quartet

for I. X.

I

orpheus' endearing secrets have been bestowed on Aïs

. . . ascending the rhythm of resurgent arrows
towards her, hers . . . a million and one fractured pulses
carved in music

II

its major chapter quickened his narration
resuming its self-surrender, lambent over him
its minor edge has reappeared

written against hope 'the trial of a quest' conjures
your name fair Eury-dice

III

. . . music is given over to its folds of darkness –
shrill by shrill outrageously condensed in a short duration
of timelessness

calibrating its rumbling maze . . .
at all hazards striking to the beat of silence . . .

IV

rose-fingered Greece subtracts

sedate lilies in lineal perspectives
white carrion lips piercing through the moon
and craving for it

cyme phocaea smyrna priene miletus, ephesus . . .
fostered by the ottoman rape

having retained unaccountably the compass of Apollo
on the bias of her aeolian chart

22 quintet

I

death rattle's segregated purity

enraged at clarion consonants near and far voiced aloof

speared with piercing vowels . . .
reverberating upon maddening echoes . . .
contagious to *maenads singing*

II

aphrodisiac

having nothing allowed for the tremens of impotence
which water-snake . . . sex in denial
incensed to revoke enticements or fear . . .
abides unrecalled

III

itching for a forbidden flush in hearts, subversion is
                                        abandoned
(threatened with wild jokers for the remainder of the hand
        by abstruse winners' truant lovers
aces in disguise 'saw me')

IV

beware

promiscuously racked with honeyed stings
Oedipus vouched
for his dwarfish mother

nothing more emptied
from the hives of incestuous thebes

VI

but you desired again her Eleusinian mercy
older, bacchic, without home without wine
       discordant-voiced in reverie

hastily against time being set apart
       lust of my love come what may

23 quartet

I

bird of prey
    electric oresteia
(miscast in a national theatre over-production)
    hauled at the filial goal of unscrupulous memories
albeit of a poet's testicles
    as a fraction of the wholesomeness
of sexual greece

II

without provisions
she 'caters for'

indeed as often abjured from the oyster-bed
wearily porcine
she would dispatch the nimble mollusc

shrunken without recourse
abetting the emaciated dreamer
in self-squandering

III

'parting of the ways' time has been hollowed out
thoroughly 'to a fault' acknowledging subtle illusions . . .
rows of holes . . . rockboring caresses

thrust through time's perforated skin, out of the future

IV

greece

no older than the cruelty of its fate
afore held in its iron grip, no way immortal

being compared with the features of morning light
on her chiselled childhood, nobody steered again

24 quintet

I

displayed in the Humber
anchored to a vapid eel . . .

striven foghorns swollen cylinders
lingering Donna Nook Rosemary Beacon
the most secular Lower Burcom Light Float, the most lonely
East Walker Dyke Light
flashed once a minute in the green current of estrangement
at the lowest 'low death'

II

it does not matter, either in playing the game
or placed for abandon
chanceless beyond revoke under an unassailable deal
redoubling the stakes on death

III

submission

recalcitrant as a muzzled foreigner
whose mongrel's sucker am i
ungrudgingly roaring in silence

not amiss – being led to stultifying safe-conduct
'a dog is not safe to touch'

IV

my only love the trawler 'nothing off' . . .
upbraided (by the cod-faced) for his birthright . . .
shackled to the nets of foul deposits
hauled at a furious pace below bare grounds
no nothing

V

it was as if they banked on a surplus inundation
and would wager against damned swindlers
when the oily blanket slipped over rival traffickers
(fishing) in the rapid water

25 quintet

I

nothing is a given to speak of 'a straight rape'
'if you would show an enraged adolescent
under a sickening body – how you pitied him
trouncing his opening bid'

II

   compulsorily either to reckon
from the tidal hand of dispensation
   two for twenty one, death and desire if dealt a pair
or fear has given its show away over a wicked smile

III

besides permeating through its hoarse lamentations
she would have suckled a gravid mare's blood-bounty

as if being enraptured by fear
at the likeness to his disembowelled horse

IV

bestrode on its eleusinian victim
fire coming in between male waves to perform
revenged on the glaswegian hermaphrodite

white bosomed with fear for its sickening harbinger
of deadly ashes, charity stooped, in care

V

why ever did you condense the tacit choir's strokes
of blood, offering no apology
putting out to tender the extra beefy boy's
celestial agent, encompassed behind an abstinent lover

26 quintet

I

thriftlessly in debt
the king of diamonds declared
a secret relish for bankruptcy

   with pertinent humour
reaching the maximum of a two-way affair
placed for death's double indemnity

II

self-begotten as an ethereal somnambulist
he hanged himself at the marginal bulwark . . .
distraught by the hook of moribund dreams . . .
repeating his lunar somersault – into oblivion

III

dartboard

he aimed for a near miss at the elusive treble
poverty's ill-joined deceptions maddening in their truth

(the bullseye's chaos has been covered, no uproar
   no underwhelming target chosen)

IV

why did you submit to a troddenheaded doggerel
if not to traffic in money-grubbing . . .
    bewilderingly for gratuitous pursuits
even if the body-blow seemed a trifle vicious

V

    obliquely in the manner of st john the baptist
ill-humoured salome was beheaded

    ensnared in error in the haven of love
reclining full-length from her sensual detour
    to his mischievous priestliness

27 quintet

I

donald crowhurst

north by north east below visibility
Teignmouth Electrons to Electra
becalmed even in the wind

every twenty seconds a flurry of music shook with her
chargeable to her biassed course
in the unquiet stone of darkness

II

(ostentatiously dreaming
you shouldn't swear to a light-heeled fantasy
thereafter spoken in riddles
against the knight-errant's hurtling undertow)

III

in default of homesickness neither here nor there
seeking out a traverse
adjacent to stifling ulysses
shoals of racing shadows lengthened to a white skyline . . .
fugitive memories running over each erroneous coordinate

IV

orphic to the point of insanity
   I staked my life on a pair of dreams
without redoubling against losing
while picking up two more convulsions
   and raising death by one

V

at breakanchor of death on the rebound
she overhauled her swilling overtures
offering the gulls' imagery for the iron lining
of her scraping ribs –

surreptitiously washed by the sun
shackled to a frenzied sea-cloth
to the leeward of her breakage

28 quintet

I

olympian I

would we have ridden over her chasing death
involved in a ravaged face-off

securing a wager to win on her maiden debut
while in mourning – unacquainted with her silence

II

why confer a foul on the cradle-goal of a roused player
narrowly emulous of the winner's cheeky sham

what's the fire-drake's dividend
in cowering his aphrodisiac shimmer
striking at a thousand and one afflictions
for the ribald penalty

III

drawn to the frowning at victory
embracing olympian dissentient nemean
degenerate mock-rebellious shivering flames blasted
though never mind – the dexterous wag missed by inches

IV

in the patient bowling the bruised batsman
spurned a brilliant encounter

hitting an outside leg virgin ball

nothing else he confutes of the fair canon
at his barren crease

V   .

the bastard striker has run with a break-neck sagacity
exuding a headyflying grace and a delphic melancholy

lest you'll vow 'unfair your penalties'
his feet'll turn to stone

29 quintet

I

withernsea esplanade

shamelessly given to cuddling
'will you wash my blood away'
    veered off in quest of the spilling breakwater
urging a crimson seagull to murder

II

    strike-bound
whatever abridgment gorged her sail
her madness was to command

moored in chilling irons in a beaten strait-jacket
hinged on her strait-laced rope
    foul green and unattended

III

in mid channel – from a flying trapeze
in the likeness of a wreck
surmounted with balls wallowing downwind
at the bottom of the rubbing sea
your father pulled the trigger

now where the azure undertaker cast anchor

IV

my mother vouched for the seagulls' emperor
uncompromisingly on fire imbued with peer gynt

yet only on the circling ice the scalded current
prefigured her leaden breakage

V

what would it have been for a homeward dog to follow askant
won't it take you in the smeared moonlight
thoroughly barking at its idle rest

brick-moulded in her lime spitting kiln
could it have begun again at my mother's interment

30 quintet

I

being had, you laid open the wondrous fairground
ejected from rainbowed vowels
in the opposite direction of the mountain dew
without an alibi for the mucus injuries
in the aberrant verdure anticlockwise to the coalface
they took their own lives

II

towards the Hebrides, Eurydice not yet countercharged
drew no acquittal from the navigator's child

windward it surrendered her blood-curdling compass
headlong – fluctuating on the lyre's steering axis

III

at the ore-hewed island you voiced fortune's incandescent
telling, bursting at the seams of the scuttled circumflex
of sorrow   (thereby hangs a cymric wreck
caulking up the plainsong of mercy killing)

IV

thesoulofengland

it gathered speed as it were bid my dear
    self-styled, boyish . . .

no longer engulfed in his silty mane
    flying over the dormant ground

pursuing his indignant lover
    over a foreshortened distance
of time

V

abruptly Desert Orchid falters

at all hazards in the silver air
as if his flight never at rest

'sparkling white flower'
trounced the heart of Cheltenham

31 quintet

I

you added no hope to the pool of life
   my darling caliban

ariel was found amassing the oily prowess of treason
his wings channelling a beacon of blood

ran amuck per capita
   my darling caliban
succinctly questioned the waste

II

st john allegedly burrowing in silent meadows
into eruption

fractional noises . . . who stabbed his own sonofabitch
whose unconvincing tears . . . swayed in revenge

III

he lost sight of the apollonian ship

abreast of her redundancy . . .
from a bloodandthunder high-water mark
bloodthirsty impoverished dogs' elegiac injuries
eyes in teeth unskilled to cry
raging at her punishment

allotted to paraphrase her requiem
   'what's the uncharted news'

IV

had I have seen a sunrise without the sun
   crying out 'Punch the great'

the killer child fought
   red vomit hardens

V

as soon as Judy contrarily humpbacked destroyed her
                                        trappings
ostensibly gouging out her wrestling child
pampered in injury-time's rehearsal on a margin of error
   the skipping rope hauled off her forehead

32 quintet

I

starvation encroached on cecilia, pulling in jest
a senior ass, six billion dividends for beggarly headstrong
iniquitous overtimers risen above the burnished corridors
with ghostly immediacy redeemed their losses

II

on my tenth birthday, being sold beastly reformed
    hollowly smitten with dear life
'the glacial boulder will pardon you
    the streets will assign you'

III

the rubber condom in chiaroscuro dried
painted against hallowed gas, crack-addict virgin MARY
                                          spouts
defeat, strangers of no less intimacy looked away

gouging out a tear
irreverent in its perspective

IV

like someone who breaks in
through the grinding air
under concrete walls
like someone fleeing from every corner
oberon junked her needles

like a veinstruck beggar
titania bore down on her purple limbs

V

homicidal orpheus encompassed your table . . .
his iridescent exploits redundant . . .
dowsed with coltrane's steely segments . . .
in token of the bearings in music

33 quintet

I

cricket

the bowling changed

hopelessly, for the farthest outfield . . .
their batsman blocked in resplendence

as a riotous child 'rattles the sabre' wishing the ashes

II

maiden over

a well crafted ball
reveals its demeanour

softly under compression
an upright floating wrist
carved out the lovely maiden . . .
over

III

the batsman cheated by the bounce of the ball
by the by . . . had killed us all

likely, with a bloated vagueness
resistant to chance unawares
laid into the ghost of stoic impartiality

IV

whereas we lied about adjourning for a moist recess
each dog-violet has taken shelter
throughout infringed by the lure of the ashes
– bawling, at lords we drew

V

stumped in extremity, in other grounds
it might be a memory afar

batting a shorter distance towards a forlorn angle
a few inches to nowhere

cyprian quartets

'setting out from the coast of Cilicia
towards the south,
you discover the beauty of the island of Cyprus . . .'
Leonardo da Vinci

Windsor: Dr. 12591 r. verso: notes on Cyprus
and the Legend of the Sirens c. 1508

20 july–14 august 1974

extra-time's play desists
gracious Cypris 'all heart hands and knees'

cannily tackled on broken up ground, off-side . . .
having surrendered to a vicious collision
with barefacedness

quartet 1

I

Macaria

amorously across poetry, rocks, shoals, banks
scudding in silence through a sheet at anchor

arranged for iceblink flowing syllables, 'Cy-pris'
deemed unruffled on the star chart . . .
drifting over the cruellest of deaths

II

the rape of Cyprus

'sell dear' for a final price
by a compass-bias shown to rejoice in a race
on no account won
'Nicosia-Engomi-Dhekelia'
dearest CYPRUS   unduly scattering her total
adrift . . . in hell's current

III

Kytherea Aigialousa Salamis
(each has drowned in herself)

intrepidly in love with sea-borne, dry-lodging Cyprian –
her curse upon my heart's unbroken yearning

IV

ousted from chaste Kyrenia
will the moon confound its lingering memento of war
will a deep-cut VENUS surrender to anybody's
inept conscience notwithstanding laying hands on her

quartet 2

I

buffer zone

pollen's fecundity has been reproduced
at variance to its destruction
     Cypris . . .
scanned by war's facsimile – lying abruptly to herself –
is growing farther estranged

II

retentive of betrayals
endowed with the auburn features of the night . . .

lovers who have endured 'the game killed'
disparaged, old, puckered to a fault,
relapsed

ushered in brutal rejoicings
unforgettable shreds . . . stood in the breach

III

the satyr of 'Cyprus vivant'
is indeed put out to pasture

(a stricken saint
hysterically under the pretence of remaining still
alludes to salvation

unedited corpses shielded by the nearby grass)

IV

Tilleria – after Kon Ichikawa

twenty four similes at war as of a siren
were released
vehemently mutilated images
lying open on fire
wrapt in skeletal blossoms . . .
but why?

quartet 3

I

Dhekelia

unforgivingly Cyprian – under its bridal spears
the grounded moon deployed the lagging sun
having mistaken its unrevoked brilliance and flair

enlisted his exhumed eclipses and dying rays

II

as ever wrought, white-copper tears
are Helen's apprenticeship with Venus

bronze-blue, retaliated upon crescent Cyprus
against the ancient torso of her coast

as yet held dear by her rapists
as now assaulted by passive music

III

ravaging St Thyrsus

assiduous Turks might amble home
    without reserve
(having declined no plausible latitude
    in a clandestine change-over
for a proper exit)
    – secure in holding the outer station

IV

Cyprus' ransom-bond

who divested himself of a crushing defeat

will barbedwired Venus
    without limbs
'stand by'

will a subdivided crew drown together
    to pick up the ancient stroke
of freedom

slithery blades were mishandled at the redoubt

quartet 4

I

(after 'the beheading of St John the Baptist'
by Caravaggio)

licentious in so far as to ruminate on the embittered
feast's sagacity
St John the Baptist, an aphrodisiac youth
his irreducible aura and disquiet
beheaded for its decorum
on an elegiac painting about love

II

he severed the colour from its shadow
    notwithstanding a Hellenic intolerance for suffering
he assigned to the wounds
    shared by 'St John' and his decapitated future
he whose twilight failed butchery

III

Ammohostos – the closed city

'AMMOHOSTOS my love unbound' I cried
incensed by the dormant void, jeered at for bubbling over
perhaps being miscast in the recurring plot

gnawing at a frenzied revulsion for its Aeschylean pangs
of such ruin

IV

being held in its terminal sneer
at the cloistral heap of lulled creations
time is hindering redemptions

(as with a prayer's invariable mourning
for enclave AMMOHOSTOS . . .
undelivered from the arms of Morpheus) . . .

quartet 5

I

what cheer?
the dinner party cut in
fallaciously ratified by hunger

cradledwithknives – she, Aphrodite of Soli
picking at the pieces of the infernal
meat's lusciousness

II

St John the Baptist opened the ball
she, swinging straight through on the rise of a kiss
poised at head's level

he, the beheaded dancer held sway
as far as the farthest reaches of memory
spring from

III

oh Kyrenia

death doubled the stakes

while impaled on the moon in reverie
standing pat on hope
'no, nor half a life'

for the odds on chance to re-raise
are a given – imponderable

IV

Lycophron – Alexandra

ill-spoken of Cypris
on the verge of raucous inflections
transmitting shrills for war

given as a bias in solitary dances
masculine voices extended across
a song cycle of rattling urgency

quartet 6

I

[*this section is missing or was never completed – ed.*]

II

status quo

how many more derisory games
are played out on a recalcitrant maxim
what matters a wherefore?

how many remaining Troys
repeating the token of their dissolution

how much inexorable hatred
uncompromising in an eruption of death
abruptly resumed its course of moribund place

III

Irish odds

it's just a matter of bluff, isn't it?

a fallen petal threatens . . . a martial iris withers . . .
a poor osseous hand has been abandoned

'beaten by their own rites of war' . . .
as the death song of Ossian – folds
without tenderness

IV

thirty and one thousand tyrants

anew a nonentity
surreptitiously glorified

devoid of soul, breath, reason, understanding
yet again an illicit solace indecorum
to be reckoned with

quartet 7

I

our entertainment has fallen short of choice
jealously nibbling at laughter's tears . . .

hammered out in awe of Cypris, goddess of hatred
unheedful of pretence, my ludicrous darling

II

he declared war against
destitute Cypris – a queen needed
for an elusive straight

sour as a drunken troubadour
he stayed in
his lust all out for the maximum pot

'confounded no longer'

III

worthless Aphrodite

erroneously held dear for a melancholic kiss
(sensually tantamount to bluffing)

she will then have 'stood on'
two hearts towards rejection
self-impotent beyond revoke

IV

surcharged by five irregular diamonds
indeed the Turk was unencumbered

full-house-affluent
otherwise transfixed on saturated flesh
will he straddle the Cyprian prey

quartet 8

I

who might vote in –
the shreds of democracy

under a near Aristophanian cloud
azure arsed wartsandall
lying barren in the womb of chaos

contemptuously air guitar playing
        Socrates
launched into derision

II

in disquiet at fear's brutal rot, hellish incest endures
to remonstrate upon 'an unbridled blood's tortuous streaks'

written out in token of lust
'how grossly you loved me'

III

in mid navel

a Babylonian rose languishes in the desert

engulfed in oil
swirling under its weight

several petitioners
– in retreat –
giving credence to the residue of war
(negotiating death with a simpleton enemy)
hazarded stasis

IV

Persian echoes

allusive to the pious anger of 'Paradise Lost'
I forswore the ruffians to demob

as the unreckoned agent of uncompromising fate
having blown myself up

in the least best moment

quartet 9

I

the rhetoric of war

if captives of hawknosed words
    prying into their tongues' shortest defeats
spoke – would they succour with expiring lips
    eloquent scaremongers
to requite for a triumphal repartee

II

    what a resplendent dislike
due to insidious controversies
    whereby foul play interlocked with its solsticial villainy
blindly reached me

III

I wish I had no relish for boredom
by the by I was spoken to thus O thus
  'stave off'

brewed with the groans of ennui
familiar to an extinguished Arcadia
(if unbecomingly being enchanted by similitudes)

IV

fear allowed pleasure to dwell in me
(as a startled child benumbed of underground fetishes)

through untrodden bypaths – still unreflective
on inescapable images . . .
GALATEIA LAPATHOS MORPHOU . . .

quartet 10

I

the flesh of England

'what's all this in aid of?'
endeared to money being counted out under the scare of
                                        lacerated trivia . . .
fleeting expressions of impeachment levered over . . .
preposterously lashed against my fingers' oarlock

II

vanity bequests have been reshuffled over and over

eager to begin changing resolutions
– white offal, rotten by repute 'checked'
the decomposed 'lady of the lake'
again demurred

III

the Annan plan

in the manner of gin rummy
the heart's villain
followed suit of an English 'cri de cœur'
(in plaintive Greek)

each player scores anew
– inexorable points for every atrocity won

IV

Richard Dadd – a travesty

Crazy Jane's intoxicating mass is tinged with murder . . .
fairy dilutions' tonal washes are drying out
white, off-rose reflections . . .
wallowed in her underbelly's scarlet undertow

delusive mirrors enticing her – cracked
with filial brutality

quartet II

I

coastal energy

while starved – to rot into perversity
ill-gotten, threatened with howling seagulls
wrangling about their countermove, bathed in oil
I breathe in death's carrion exuberance

II

asylum seekers

placed on the 5 red
chance losing hold of tomorrow wounds itself into
                                             oblivion

rotating impartially in fabulous disguise
in the face of its artificial glitter – opposite to zero

III

fear's vexation muscled in . . .
the carcasses of the asylum seekers lay afloat . . .
pursuing their second circular route
of undeclared infighting

IV

(prematurely stoic in the wake of violence)
dreamers unruled beyond controversy
struggling in the direction of the asylum's bluster
canned on infusible passions . . .
will not be accepted

quartet 12

I

for a cause

as ever yet so beautiful, eaten by death
languid without a hitch in the random front line
– apart from being disingenuous – brewing rebellion
as never again atoned for, to hand – so wombless

II

'it augurs ill' . . . the oracle of war wastes
   woman and child, delphian in motion

repeatedly being solicited for its dispatches
   to the core of obscenity . . . insulting music

III

flag of truce

why so many euphemisms about 'hawking up'
why so many inverted syllables

sneered at the rebus of unfair melancholy
why, so to abet the fountain of cruelty

IV

(incoming administration)

death's bilious revenues
have been gathered in crummy disrepute

second per second . . . lickerish terriers
digging a bias for prudent mongrels

contritely outmanoeuvered
in rescuing an infectious bulldog

modern Greece

Euterpe

la fille de joie

post-nuptial Greece
altering course . . .

scudding to windward of arion, she, with dolphins
note after note, coils further away

the rickety compass slackens

she, the bride of the luscious seas
falsely navigating at random

quintet 1

I

Lasus of Hermione

music
has given voice to rattling Greece
as a love song

listen
remember me to the sirens

incomprehensibly echoing
death's dance poem . . .
            – fractured in joy and lament
aroused even

hear the breach of silence
reverberating upon 'lasus of hermione'
(he, the precursor of translucent harmonies)

II

a cadence befell on Athens
music is my own turbulent city
lying enclosed
east by west

disjunct from her own birthright
hostage to her youth

cymean consonants, female vowels
aeschylian chords . . .
strikingly hemmed in silence

reaching in cyclic annihilation
the slaughtered larynx of Apollo

III

newbuild white haired Greece
summons betrayal
to lay its most barren foundations
in music

wire-wrapped cyprus
corrupted voiced
modelled on its notation
of death

strained under the remnants
of a wiped out melody

kassandra's forward path

IV

eager to peruse the ratio of Greece
in music playing
I stopped

mapped out in current rhythm . . .

amputated fingers, lips sheered off
improper fractions of a non-emotion

astray in the direction of 'no thoroughfare'
codifying Helen
into a perfect lapse

V

far purer, scrutinized
as her own corpse
eludes decay

as a grecian voice by birth
although it retains
the tremulous features
of chaos

bound up with clear Ionian syllables
absorbed into time's invisibility
an ulcerated hellene
is washed in rhythm

quintet 2

I

at the outer door
random Iphigenia in Aulis
was procured

time-dishonoured
transferred into another unknown inner-city
gratis for her fragmentation

floor-tapping, finger-snapping
a total revenge

II

serial Bacchus
betokens ancient bouts
of music

a Dionysian stir of manhood
gradually . . . unceremoniously
suppressed
under the weight
of his own rocking body's
heat and fire

so calm, so riddled with dissembling impetus

III

Lysistrata confounds unbending
the spatial tedium
of noise makers
'bewildered bacchic goats
written over
surplus music
against their war'

she, virtuoso to a fault
raging mad
limb-relaxing
in phallic Athens

IV

poverty-stricken Euterpe

as a consensual synthesizer . . .
the Aristophanian nightingale's
inexhaustible syrinx
struck bewilderment

(switched on by a nearly ostinato silence . . .
while filtered through the digital babel's
propelling clouds)

never relinquishing
its ethereal vigil of music

V

'aeitho'
he indulged
in the sound of the feminine letter e . . .

g   r   e   e   c   e
it augurs well for music

'eros'
swamped in an uncompromising shade
of antiquity
has risen to fall

he, whose inheritance
of autumn leaves
is enshrined in harmony

quintet 3

I

the english horn rejoiced
at its own militant prize
bloodcurdling . . .

aural displays of terror
overblown . . .
from one slaughtered deer to another
(alias the transposing instruments
of diminished pastures)
a shire as beautifully sacrificed
as greece scored for
'iphigenia in tauris'

II

bisexual apollo
he, an atheist priest
imperceptibly ostracized love's abandonment

a host to st cecilia in armour
he, perhaps in defiance of the Athenian paean
in heavenly America
ordained

musical cerberus . . . barking a war

III

anew greece lengthens its silence
    wrapped in time's
conflicting density
(she, perhaps contrarily to herself
at the wedding of melodious cypris
struck at peleus and thetis' feast
    of love)
growing rich on the barest
    memory

IV

seminal death

anew
the rudder swung amuck

amidships
circumnavigating the music
of the gorgons

implicit in maria callas' softer edged
medusas

an inaudible greek
hauled down fate
for its very loudness

V

love's knots
masses of words
hinged on a bias
of weakened colour

as tense greek light
rapidly before losing its way
is drawn in

(in lieu of dark oresteia
remonstrating on its deflection
from unrelenting shadows)

quintet 4

I

la fille de joie

(my father dionysos no longer is the guardian of the
distraught)

another strenuous vacuum coaxed together its final seventh
   music endures its nemesis
in no haste silence is scattered at random

   conspicuously near and far
white hyacinths laid bare in ravaged eleusis
   compact with prostitution

II

(dreaming of the Aeolian nightingale
and its abandon in sweetness)

hauled upon
forsaken propontis . . .
a bridge to a sea of songs . . . euxine pontos
   . . . sinopi, ilium . . .
raving mad asia minor
echoing off . . . 'kemal's blood modulation'

alike thrown into confusion
I have tasted the bitter honey
of sapphic greece

III

'ravished
tenedos . . . imbros . . .'
death's solo
has been prolonged

heinous shrills
sweeping across the seized islands . . .
disbanded

(she, whose crystal reflection
capsized in the violet depths of the aegean)

IV

had we have chosen exile
while the ship's bearing falters

(tarbarrelled
swamped with music
'a child's death fugue'
stove in
its darkest fate

smyrna's
long held quavers
reiterated by each terror-stricken counterpoint
on fire)

V

in full swing
greece has given birth to
the syllables of music parenting romanos

(a practised grinder of stringed waves
 . . . sharpened into silence)

simultaneously through the prism of degenerate
Byzantium
sotiria bellou's children lament

two cinema sextets

sextet 1

I

oh dear odessa's silver nitrate
starting block
an illusion, it's 'dogged as does it'

as per usual
who is who per art
to saturate
in excess
of a bum-steer

whirring insatiably
its political burr

filmed
into oblivion

II

on course, startled

butting over
ugh, I moan

ugh, I lettered in words' loose use
I & U

what is mine – won't be yours

a soul among the night
'foot it'

but tell me oh, 'boo hoo'
the reason for our incompetence

we, embroiled in incompetence
whoops! so glad to be quit of the walls in us

III

suppose   mrs   catherine's   egg,   shoo!

  how do you?
          I have enjoyed it
          yellowish white
          like pigeons woo
          soft or hard!

O my heart

o'er tears she peers
          mrs catherine
          shoots

suppose a screened warring cock
          or canned
oh dear, dissolved her roost

'in between thes' long intervals'

IV

to an' fro
standing off
queuing up to dream
jessica keep aside an eye

there are reasons for unreason
wealth
waiting
bring forth your purse
come thes' dreams
come oh! futility, come
to lilies' lips

'ell in no time prosperity will rebound
upon our billions

eh, jessica

V

O truth
come to my arms

arms sale
ruth, the truth

of each to each
to reach a close-up's wholeness
thos' whos' hearts
're in the know

butchered at random
in a blank space
o' millions . . .

ruth, weep

for a heap of reproaches
yon wisdom of quivering heights

VI

O bellicose
acquaintance of a snack hour's
fervent recall
O on the spree a wingless
life's bitter cast
being of repair, cheer up
ther' at the bar

a butterfly, subversily, she
up in arms 'stood on' fear

him whom she accosts she dies with

sextet 2

double-dealing words
– obliquely brought into focus as a refractive sheen –
belie lies

I

on course, far gone
'nothing are thee to me'

whoops!
we for ourselves
ugh, I mourn

poverty-stricken by a soul's foot unto the night
ugh 'bear in hand'

indebted to each other, but me 'no buts'

(our departure from unrequited dreams
is setting off alone)

II

wooing a vice per device
who is who per art's rake

to deliver the share of its burden . . .

alas clickity clack art's infinitude
how does it do it

oh dear, a reality of illusions
a bum-steer
it is 'dogged as does it'

oh dear is it much of an art
damn! fair do's

III

as a rose being forged
she bled

alas, an overawed rebellion
a counter-claim
thrown to the dogs . . .

assumably
beneath a glaring error
what a sucker
gnawing away like a loafer
to strike a route

IV

couched in 'us'
  'in each other's arms'
whoops! amid a twist of the wrist

  ugh, what's ours
minus the soul of the night
  O hardly the amount of our introspection
fused to a blank

  poured out in 'us'
ugh, self-consuming
  the body breaks off

V

between us, setting out on course
ugh, I chew the rag
so absurd in our drivel, whoops!
'we' being deduced from 'us'

O, be patient, 'quite up in the air'
our own heat and dust are beaten

(whatevcr happens,
will our stumbling-block utter a dreamlike silence?
oops! 'we' so wrapped up in 'us')

VI

whatever may be the cause of our rejoinder
I mourn for neither we nor us to linger on

chicken-hearted, a rift in the night opens between us

our very soul fused to the claws of a dove
whoops! it is wanting

the relic of our departure in dreams, ugh
as rotten from without as within, oops!

made alive

the rights of sanctuary

4 Aristophanian quintets

i held the cards
reluctantly right, wrong-footing the air

with a bonus of mere aristophanian expediency
clouds up
bluffing the spiteful gamblers into melancholic raises

quintet 1

I

for the last hand
i considered the chips
more than my own death's 'all in'

while hoping against hope
the money
was retained
with impunity

II

money down
self-effacing queen high peers over shadows
to get the hump about and fold

phallic spades up reads despair
unvaryingly matching the chances

III

'are the odds incalculable . . .'
in what order of time does death warm
in which hidey-hole are the stakes over

askance losing out on false impressions
a queen of spades eludes your icy hand

IV

keep in suspense 'face downwards'
the impish joker

or rather at a disadvantage without precedent
conned, diamond jack
notwithstanding the rules of fear 'stood on'
aimlessness

V

he has drawn to sensual pleasures
while ousting the honey queen

she. self-righteous for outmanoeuvred temptations,
virtuously called by a pair of hearts to a flush
raised her body

quintet 2

I

for alex higgins

intractably (on oath
of cueing superbly)
hitting the first lightning-stroke into an ordered mass
covered by death
although the Attic Frogs have never framed the balls

II

in our earlier play your fingers rolled on me
hauled down on the barren score of my conscience
in the waspish light of a thwarted form
stricken across that late oneupmanship
cueing amorously alone

III

pocketed slantingly with a cushioned knock
knuckled under at a distance
see how i began the break

plucking death's balls out of their spotted virginity
wholly in love

IV

pointless by half, i nudged the ball into an abyss
pocketing my heart and cueing off its shadow

akin to – by default to snooker behind love's limit
are you the winner at this final frame
am i not ashamed

V

ascribed to your defeat
short of dying
good day to you

like a chicken with one leg
likewise broached at the point of a variant pot
of similes unchecked
the bold-rope of harmony snapped
the balls veered and stalled

quintet 3

I

at the rocky bottom of the table, i confounded a man in love
as outfaced by blindness as I – eyeball to eyeball
baulked at his safety

on a winking coastline
his right eye was glancing higher than my own left
and it wanted me

II

irreversibly at stake i'll in turn stink of money
    forcing the pot to cushion the odds

running at spotted shame, pool's fugue simulates the ball
    disorderly struck misbegotten
'bridged by counterpoint'

III

pink over the pocket
he had the coward's option to cue askew

or for this kin of triumph – strikingly pocketing the cagey
                                                    plant
in spite of a lesser acquittal

IV

alex head high in shame in liquid fire
had need to reassert his potting
    counterbalanced with icy thoughts
or rather playing with safety
'losing a life' cueing over aristophanian balls in baulk

(perhaps to snooker himself
    by another freak vagary)

V

the next in order challenged by the divinity of winning
ominously beaten at a distance
atoned for his disputed variant of losing

he pockets the balls . . . death cues in cycles

quintet 4

I

Greek roulette

cowardly allusive to the myriad futile undertakings
i am devoted to

greed and wealth are spinning about

encumbered with each high-flown initiation rite
at the wheeltheball theslots of either's wishful harshness
adherent to too many

II

strike-bound, the ball declined to rattle
(inverse lysistrata)
grumbling if the spin revolves to retreat further off
at the contrary of what it is expected to secure

– predestined for war against the wheel's atrocious sexuality

III

for a trillion on zero
there is no limit to hope

glowing green, a null parity of boundless slots
deserted a chance that might have been
but it is not – the chariot of fate

very nearly circumscribed
the minimum on Greece

IV

mock philocleon

stung deadly amiss at zero

chips anew were placed on obsessive erotic injuries –
split bets on wasps against my father
for a kiss onto his mouth
abiding unaltered

(remember the payoff is as ever
with the house)

V

askew democracy bidden to the roulette wheel obliged
as if it was redoubtable for a violation of injustice to fall
into the grip of chaos

bet odd greek . . .
but 'grin and bear it'

words on poetry

in emerging from
as in the task of writing
we rise from fear,
still more fearful

words on poetry

the prejudice in favour of innocence
contrarily forged in eloquent guilt

the fallacy of the eternal, the pure and the beautiful
precipitated an excess of alike beliefs as in a rose

or – as if by default – beguiled by verse –
a certainty, a truth (being) made verse

whether words
(in the context of nature
or in their elements)
are likened to the feminine form
the poet decides

to which
idle death had the language of memory
resorted? As in the future tense
       – will engender –
hence a crawling intimacy – upon words
a forsaken birth – enduring – in poetryhood

the application of vision by the adjective
the colour of the sky – bespoke in syllables –
silence its plaint
may compound poetry . . .

severed from –
adverse to tenderness – conjoint lust
poetry in denial – he, she, it

are uttered as instances of one and the same

risen from, fallen into languor, perhaps delineate verse
    ascending – into frailty

oblivion recalled by the souvenir of poetry
    anew dissolved

perhaps I had to submit to a morbid choice of words verse

kursk

69°40′N 37°35′E

15 quintets & 2 quartets

each beam of the baltic moon
bore witness to dima kolesnikov's
sumptuous death

Kursk 12 august, 2000

dima's note

'it is dark to write here. but
i'll try by the feel of touch
it looks like there are no chances to get out
10 − 20%
let's hope at least someone reads this
here are the names of the compartment's submariners
some will try to escape . . .

greetings to all
don't despair, kolesnikov'

quintet 1

I

whose body reclined in her soul
hauled up by one mortal call

the fiery dragon vouchsafed no answer

bottomed at 12,000 degrees fahrenheit
kursk's golden section
convergent to her nuclear vigil

II

S.O.S. damn it to hell

gennadi lyachin patron saint of the kursk
whose mournful voice intoxicated by its total abstinence
wedged open the throat of heaven
as one sinner in remission
'S.O.S. . . . damn it to hell'

III

as a child
i endeavoured to aggregate the ominous scores

war-fetishes
cunningly swarming with their wreckage
aping virtually whom

unmuzzled images of death
rebound at me

IV

at one fell swoop
the kurskian moon has risen

its rueful sheen silted up –
he himself debating its flawed rays

scoffing thoroughly at an unsummoned course
unkind to him

V

would you let me go cheap

whether as a self-absorbed ghoul fooling around
or cast aside
for having ceased to remit
a mock-penury
(so often called death's bonus)

quintet 2

I

the fat boy

let fly at the kurskian bulk

charred eyelids ejecting tears
most tenderly keen violet green
were handled by the moon

let fly at the sea's knight in arms
set on fire by 'death's fuel, death's soul'
nuclear fat, dulled in succession

II

nuclear Persephone put forth herself
a leafless ocean
capriciously unseasoned underfoot
at random dreaming of the right of way underground
to the undertow of the abyss

III

death's traffic in the barents shallows
rejoiced
in its uprising

it sucked at the carrion
of one mock flower

remitting fair
pervasive hues
coarse in adversity

IV

to whom is the barents sea most indebted
    for its turmoil

she on fire, shadowed out with undimmed reflections
obliterating medusa's answer

V

trumped!
set in place
on the lowest ice-ledge
under her mutinous lips
entombing the 15 men
in the two nuclear reactor
compartments

foreshown in terror
dogged by an alien memory
far away

quintet 3

I

a voice was maimed

aspirant to st cecilia
death ruffles her keel

speared with the evening light
steering through streamlets of dance

unfathomed speed and depth
'blown in'
with a striking drop and a turn

in no doubt about her course towards nowhere

II

recumbently silent
she switched to the opposite direction of life

no longer vying with her fire-darkened children
to reinvest for a kindred pushkin in need

III

bathed in vidyayevo . . .
she battened down the hair of the gorgons

enduring on a gleam of hope
a spring-wish that murder will out

contemptuously wishful of its respite
having disposed of the memory of ithaca

IV

by and by it slackened off . . .

the fire-shaven moon
by its aptitude for vacuum
unresistingly contagious to suffering

knotted to her wooing sensuality
'kursk's onrush of death'

V

i melded the bodies together onward
in their rummy sequence

laid down the singed joker
in exchange for one or more barents death
as a saving grace

quintet 4

I

at Zapadnaya Litza

gnawed mute in fear
had i dreamed of you
in the liquorish air

(would a wanton silence with any grace
rise for a fall)

on gusty boundaries
fairly tearing off

as amorous as the wind
beats its breast

II

distracted from 'hoping against hope'
gaseous airs and shadows impinged on fire
to wander off

not without precedent
o fair KHALIMA ARYAPOVA
a body's contour
abides by the desert's offhand salvation

III

dearest, mourn not death's recurrence

S.O.S. . . . frightful melodies
heavily gunned with tears under the searing barents
held sway unsolaced . . . after a northernmost
'shostakovitchian recall'

IV

submersible portraiture

(no escape occurs) from the umbilical cord

inscrutably bound to one smitten submarine
water . . . fire 'hauled at kursk'
'hove to' enclosed in the shadow of time

V

twin nuclear reactors. 118 men.
one swimming pool. onboard mascots
including 24 cruise missiles. 2 torpedoes
and vasily the cat – abruptly quenched

sheathed in a mass of memories
is the tolstoyan circuit
aforesaid extinct aeolian light . . .
Baltic redundant to contend with

the explosion sends the submarine
spiralling downwards

quintet 5

I

juliet, the last escapee
opened on 'the ace of hearts' coral refuge'
irrespective of love's foundations
on death's uproar

all but an *embarras de choix*

kursk's nuclear space
dallied away . . .

II

love's rising fear
raised its hunger

congealed lips incontinent of appetite
wrongly immersed
under compulsion

exuding their morbid desire

III

one semi-bluff slithers into focus
    alternatively exposed –
in rival attraction to the unscripted lens

as many shadows were played out in fear
    intercutting
between a truant iris and its opening
    face downwards

(we are assuming that
'sunrise' is the maximum raise permitted)

IV

(Andrei Tarkovsky
says no to solitude

in one indistinct landscape's obscene ground
he checked as in a post-nuptial poker zone
to win the fungus while tender
unless a bluff)

V

12 / 8 / 2000

mockaugust is again in leaf
surging by rebuked buds
withered flowers would seem in blossom

death's odour is perpetually hostile to the seeming
and the real

she has chosen a tremulous light
   blown up by the tips of the fingers

reeled in on the cusp of darkness
   against the moon's temporary rebellion

quintet 6

I

for senior lieutenant Alexei Ivanov-Pavlov

'rode at anchor'
sailed on her lips

what matter . . .
rocking cascades of tears
pounded into nausicaa

no matter
for a sinking vessel
launched on fire
breaking off her reckless hospitality

II

while remaining motionless
between the diversion of the flames
and the variation in the mock compass
he is betokened to an ice flower

taken aback in the unnamable
current of the smoke

III

'there is a shortage of
belts and individual respiratory kits'

was death a cover up?
gathered in the swelter of ethereal carbon dioxide . . .
intangibly puckered in death

liquefied beyond revoke in one emergency escape suit . . .
may rashid aryapov rest unamazed

IV

the ancient boat bears down . . .
insanely overtaken at the stroke of
one unrecovered bowman
ice-crust oars
disused blades
'lying to'

at the arctic site of zapadnaya litsa
leaking venus . . . exuberant kursk . . .
preparedness hurtling

V

the final blast is driven
under barents

ignited kursk insuperably
riveted into
gennadi lyachin's aeschylean affinities

quartet 1

I

kursk's wager of fireworks has been straddled
'death's up'
she, keeping vigil in rude anticipation
of bluffing
having thrown a poor hand in
– in unrestrained concealment

II

reaching towards tomorrow's stint of timelessness
like NIKE UNFASTENING HER SANDAL
feet and toes scattered

she, kursk on a hiding to nothing, counterbalanced
by one too many ancient preeminences to riot

III

'deadlice'

death has been sweetened
the enchantress of the twin nuclear reactors
succumbed to one knave and a freak

Kursk 69–40N – 37–35E is warming up
hazardously upping the stakes to one tumbled corpse

(the tears of a child 'are speaking first'
intermingled with fire
laying face upwards to each silent player)

IV

all stars ran amuck in barrel-green stupor
S.O.S. . . .wateroilandfire

dear kursk

the pool was divided up
purring explosives
against carbon dioxide encroachment –
devil-driven, hollowed out
embracing all hands

for nothing other than forging ahead
in the shallows of betrayal

quintet 7

I

'cheers kursk'

on a drinking bout
whether I or he's on a fool's errand
gluttonously released
from our unsusceptible boredom
it augurs fear . . .
O how enthralling
assuming to escape
off and on – alive

II

neutralizing the archangel

of heaven kursk no longer simulates
love-set due nuclear
redoubtable to her hideous requiem

bearing in self-reproach towards the sound of fire

III

as an elusive child
biased by the stakes of pleasure

dear knows . . .
self led by fear
drawn and quartered
at child's play

let be . . . lagging after into cruel reprobation

IV

a spring wish was upheld
orphic ophelia
embroiled in the rites of profusion

discreditable kursk . . .
nuclear ophelia under cover
'heartrending' was aroused

cloaked in a waste of flagrant unguent
alias leaking gas

V

confound it, whatever happens S.O.S.
nuclear juliet ignobly
beaten by love's maximum flame

north west 'the fat boy opened with a cracked jaw'

containing her elephantoid teeth . . .
'kursk's hand, on fire' amorously came in

quintet 8

I

kursk, nymph, no matter . . .
will ever wrought melancholic eyes
reciprocate in tears

or unwillingly rummage about
the captain's daughter's seabed
among 20,000 lb of hurtling explosives

for senior warrant officer pugachev's own fire

II

nauseous games

she drew to a greater fear face upwards

kursk alias aurora
having discarded a full house in flames
as to win on the shallows of the barents sea
putting up the maximum silence

III

risking more than k. could afford to lose –

he matched the straddle in fire
having thrown in twice the amount of death
on one beaten submarine
twenty three corpses to one against the barents tumult
saying check

IV

S.O.S. . . . air water fire, nuclear
of contrary resolve . . .

she, kursk,
gathered amidst clouds
set fast in the moonlight

choose as may
we ourselves taken in – submerged together

V

no one has ever found salvation

compressed into one emergency escape suit
is he emulating the fabled halcyon optimum

for azure rashid aryapov

quintet 9

I

the gambler

turbine section – the firegorgon

she has thrown her hand in
for an insatiable monster's elimination

O how the bluffing vipers of medusa threaten
how she 'stood on' the wretched heat

her welcome resounds through the eddying frontier
'S.O.S. . . . nuclear nausicaa'

II

exhorting to recall of high diving
swirling legs and toes together
while piked of back and breast

further back under the moon

in her mesmeric endeavour
as an off-centre near liverpudlian nymph
dribbling her humour if not her fate

III

in clear water, death swam a razor-wired back stroke
life a breast rebuttal, hope a Cyprian ancient crawl

broaching the barrier to the next stage
timelessly across

IV

is the margin achieved too distant
prohibiting nausicaa's deuce

embroiled in errors
the racket buckled
over the fishermen's net

V

given the benefit of the doubt
during a precarious point of no return

in lieu of kursk's courtly nuclear strings
at love all

quintet 10

I

i would have liked
a surplus of boredom

O i was spoken to
with crossed tears
in ransom to a dumbfounded him

O i am dimpled in malaise
if ever in love
thus much in fear
of his sudden disquiet

II

coerced in fire

dear, dear, she
at the renewal of the ante
bid fair on clarion pleasures due untenable

III

viciously upping . . .
oh dear, beaten by a kiss high flush
in the orb of her sweetness

reshuffled amoretti of the maximum permissible

exposed to each other
raising kursk by one capricious mischief
razored down

IV

for senior warrant officer abdulkadr ildarov
will you reconsider your hand?

under Homeric incommunicado
pus-exhaling quasi-nuclear X is lying low
   (among unrisen heights
frantically downwards
fire opened to its own abuse)

V

what price a nuclear sub-faun?

at variance with any utopian duel
muse would be a soul, let it rest

(no thoroughfare)
highly strung – at a curve of 354 feet
adjoining infinity

quintet 11

I

(nuclear wagers were placed on arctic thebes)

Saturday 12/08/1 pm drawn to her incestuous ordeal
reproducing itself

inflammable shadows
blackfuelled, flickering bodies at full speed
outshone by fire

'opened on' one faceless carnage of dreams
wherein the innocent have no choice

II

nuclear games

at zero depth – the full house has been seen
three swindling kings accompanied by two nuclear reactors
better than three sucking pigs
escorted by two trickling queens
oh dear, tricked out of creepy similitudes

III

the carbon dioxide, the oil, its sedition
followed by sheer waste were accrued to him

towed by a dostoyevskian low hand
'a freak of death'
in bungled succession '118 inflamed waves in all'

IV

askant, coral-eyed nausicaa washed the sheets
pulled inshore at the ancient line
'let the twilight go fore'

nearly ballandsocket with a pretence of magnificence
enveloped in incestuous sands

S.O.S. . . . relayed baltic ithaca

V

(unnavigable even by memory . . . coast to coast
close hauled . . . kursk hove in sight . . .

unduly . . . east half south . . . downwards
a brace of striking lights travel on . . .)

quintet 12

I

in boredom
i wish to vouch for how
i was spoken ill of

with cross tears
in ransom to a sighing fool
'love in disguise'

O to what avail is
to swerve
from cretinous precipitations

II

what is being done
to save the people onboard?

III

'bastards'
ominously no cards exchanged –

beset by straight dealings
the king of diamonds stood pat against the queen

self-rocking, hurtling aftwards, dear, dear, she
cared for her omissions

her stake and points considered
coming upsides with fiery heavens
a middle way as yet

IV

nemesis at full blast – inverse thoughts if you will
triggering off destroyed coral's scant reflections
redpinkwhite carrion's offensive shimmer
to bear witness

V

(the bodies of the two junior torpedoists
ivan nefdekov – maxim borzhov
   are caved in)

whether bowed down by care
unmotherly drawn in harness

or whether abashed set in defiance
the moon was given its darkest kiss . . .

quintet 13

I

moskovsky komsomelets 'dammit'

as a matter of opinion
show the white feather

or death the stalker
follows on –

approaching with impending cowardice

unbearably in control
of the extent of space between

II

O scatter stars
time bowed down under its melancholic seconds
hastened in the full cycle of fear
to its risen counterpoint

III

as if kursk has been condoned
for her shambles, driven to pieces
trans-shipped on death's image
– a dumb glissando
as if it were diffused over narcissus
and bearing out his promiscuity

IV

betokened to whomsoever

dearest, listen to her confession
a plausible ante?

V

he came in – with a four inch thick layer of black rubber

he, increasing the fumed stakes . . .
she, having opened with the choking wager of her soul
for a myriad of walled tears

quintet 14

I

kursk's funeral rites – cruise missile firing

no matter, tender, tenderest these eyes keen green
    drunken aground

revengeful by a narrow margin, my poor love
    no matter . . .
tears of no weight 'buoyed up' with white flowing sheet

II

on kursk's distraught stage perished oresteian fragments
monitored the amount of silence

struck by 'S.O.S. betrayal'
forged in nuclear embraces . . .
bearing witness for a nonplus

excruciatingly encoded by a delirious liquid lustre
into the realms of tragedy

III

marine insurance

on account of the northern fleet's embarrassment
death's clusters 'stood on'

IV

'no nothing' . . .
delusive warfare emerged anew on the instant

no nothing . . . the sirens' heat deadens
'all hands' . . .

V

unscrupulously going bust for her nuclear currency
'no nothing at all' . . .

as if from under the arctic desert
the sum-remainder of the moon equals death's inflow

quintet 15

I

caught in the sacred angle of refraction
dear, dear, she
mourns over

clots of uranium . . . forgive and forget escapes me

dear, dear dima kolesnikov's bride
cajoled out of the whirling carnival
urged on such ebullience

II

death's current risen to the prurience of flames . . .
congealed amidships . . .
as forged by one disconsolate hand, self-consistent
with tapping 'S.O.S. . . . water'
– olga kolesnikov's unstoppable tears ablaze
in vengeance fell

III

k.'s first torpedo test has folded the northern fleet
a full house, knaves up (in exchange for corpses)
scheduled for mere consignment, blasted into pieces

their orphic denomination yields death's own
forsaken youth under striking water

IV

in the afterglow of kursk

(repellent water circumscribed in fire)
gluey-grey squalls . . .
simultaneously speckled
with dima kolesnikov's running sweat

V

hauled upon the rungs of the smokescreen

steeped in – within living memory
beyond the bounds of remembering

quartet 2

I

after the ante
nausicaa set on fire twenty three lives

increasingly in error, i threw in my chips

death vouched for ace low
leaking with two fates in the heart of kursk

allowing for the code of destruction, she opened
on dima kolesnikov's insoluble handwriting

II

sheering off
death began its orphic voyage
limp – mangled nausicaa
toppled over her mutilation

III

scaled up into oblivion
under a delinquent meridian

how old is the exile of memory
kindled in the furnace of racing shadows

IV

time has been noted 1 pm against zero
indelible hours . . . 'face downwards'
sub-kursk is thrown in

too late to open the ninth compartment's
charred farewell
too late, the betting before the draw is now finished

'cast off' from the vacuum of time
– time's iron-ledged inexhaustible betrayals
between monotonous bestiality and pathos
by each magnetic twist of chimeras and years
wound up in its lurid procession

remember a saying of homer's, and cherish it –
'a good messenger', he said, 'heightens
the honour of any errand.'
even the muse's stature
is more, if she be well reported.

(The Odes of Pindar, Pythian IV.XIII
tr.. C.M. Bowra)

le tableau inachevé

le tableau inachevé
(the unfinished painting)

a monologue
subsumed under a dialogue

In 1964 while a pupil at Karl Koun's theatre school, with the help of Odysseas Elytis, Iliassa distributed some copies (half a dozen or so) of *le tableau inachevé*, written a few years earlier. Iliassa translated it between 2014 and 2016.

In Iannis Tsarouchis' studio a painter friend, Bernard Eeder, added illustrations (each more or less identical) to Iliassa's handwritten text on papyrus-type rolls of paper a few metres in length. Needing funds to buy a ticket to Paris, Odysseas Elytis thought to offer copies to artist friends: Gatsos (who already knew her poems), Ritsos, Moralis and Hadjidakis may have acquired copies. She gifted a copy to Angelos Terzakis (director of the national theatre) to whom she always confided her poems. The political turmoil in Athens, close to boiling point, was perhaps a major factor in Kakoiannis and Embirikos declining the offer.

O.E. never referred to these texts on papyrus again. Soon, after a while in Paris, a welcome antidote arrived – Iannis Xenakis paying Iliassa a visit commented that the papyrus seamlessly joined the ancient with the present.

The remaining papyrus would never had resurfaced had not a copy appeared in 1991, published in *Byzantium/delirium*, an Athenian quarterly journal (now defunct), Tsarouchis having retained a roll in his studio where it languished until 1977. In London Iliassa only became aware of this through a friend. An Athenian newspaper mentions 'a bewildering monologue discovered, author unknown'.

– K.S.

le tableau inachevé

voice: A: the painter
voice: B: the unfinished painting

(emanating from the same throat)

imagine . . .

A nondescript artist's studio, off towards the right stands
an easel – a blank stretched canvas facing away from the
audience hangs on the far wall –
A soft light barely permeates an otherwise gloomy stage
from above. What prevails is the canvas, the sole element
existent. A trestle table supporting art materials and
other studio detritus is to one side

Clothed in a long hooded shroud
(face in deep shadow) the narrator stands to the front

voice A

> I was told of the present 'it must arouse your interest'
> Indeed after all I am obliged to its non future

(gesturing – seemingly towards the painting . . .)

I touch the earth . . . I peel off an unwieldy surface
wherefrom I extract a face
whose face?
to acknowledge such a semblance of another?
whose burial ground of dreams?

I stand erect on the earth
pierced with florescent lava . . .
spawned white illuminations . . . hoardings

(spoken – as struck with awe)

advertising the immortality of matter and soul

(obstinately said)

oh! dear God 'let go'

I move forward . . .
but how I conceive of a far-reaching space
as a smudge under the vaults of angels

(in a loud whisper . . .)

in the brothels I meet you
there where I reflect upon flesh
I cut into pieces its luscious carcass
money is exchanged for white dust

my canvas unravels the bodies of the dead

a reformed *poetry* greets its capital 'tenderness'
black cloth unravels the bodies of the dead

am I aware of how –
fashioned by the manner
of a nonesuch conscience –
I proceed unto the unknown – undrilled?

the same as acid-blue the water was
as bitter as laurel leaves shone. Let be

in delirium at the perplexity of how to reverse
the facts of life, each trifle in advance of itself
each of us obliquely dissipated
among jangling words
and hastened ideals . . .
the now of the present cuts across the next vacuum

– would i could only expand into the future and hope
for an unwilling world
to be revised . . .

will my own steps . . . tortuous steps . . .
press on anew forward to nowhere . . .

I was spoken to of an outer space on earth
leaning towards a remote occurrence in colour
 . . . enduring the hues of its unlikeness

will unshaken fog-bound doubts melt away?

what hope for the horizon to open up for me,

'youth against youth' is said likewise . . .
'horizon against horizon' 'hope against hope'

(abruptly)
voice B

you abandon me, a few accidental marks . . .
                                        dull-tinted . . .
or else, whose form do I wear
if not human – under a coat of rotten matter,
who am I if not the abortive visage of one's
                                        embryonic crime
red dirty foetuses ousted – bitten, motherless,
                                                fatherless

unduly reformed?

I open wide my mouth, I am hungry and thirsty

for colour, colour as a caress,
but you abandon me
searching indeed for the misnomer of 'nothing to
                                                speak of'
how far-fetched . . . the present conjoins in darkness
                                                . . . in here

this one moment resolved incomplete
is my own relic

askew, drawn on . . .
facing up to you

  perhaps a face
  – out of Velasquez
  by way of Francis Bacon
  being in love

  (have mercy on me)

voice A

  this instance will never be brought back . . . our
                                 discourse is nearly
  a 'put on' a semblance of poetry . . . imagination
                                         errs . . .

  nothing evincive, superciliously rigid, a wooden
                                   countenance
  its imageless, terminal points, 'a wreck rich in simile
                                   I dread'
  so, the eye bleeds

(always towards
the painting)

  driven away . . . apart
  'scream, tear your flesh' – wrench away the colours
  which I mixed not with matterspiritandmind as you
                               may have wished

(I created a fuss of all kinds of weapons – drugs and
                          sex) I made the colour
as shits are made, they are the refuse of our
                          LAST SUPPER
all remaining crumbs to feed SORROW,
laying out the boundary of experience, when nothing
                                        else is
in sight except you

(nearer to the painting . . .)

    triangular shapes defying the flowing curves of
                          the moon
    abrupt lines lacking the horns of perspective
    gross figurations are set against . . . 'what is to
                          be done'

    on you I placed my basic aspirations, what are they?
    suspension, suspicion, yes indeed, a great want of
                          equilibrium
    the mist, the obtuse landscapes of art, the doubt,

    death, in there I aim at – I stand erect, I step out,
                          towards, within
    narrow confined spaces . . . in there . . . whatever I do
    whatever I daub, I do it 'carried by assault'

anything more I lay to rest

gas black

4 quintets

the sky's silken dress, its pleats
bunched up by each mars violet finishing stroke
gas black, cobalt aluminate blue oblique air
roused ablaze in dry-rot intensity

bone black

I

sidewards, *permanent bone black*
death's features were preempted

(subdued *sap green*
concurrent with *brown madder* fugitive lineaments
sucked in the vehemence of time)

II

resolvent tenderness
sensuously *titanium white*
infused into sapphic *yellow ochre*

in times of aeolian redundancies
I beg of you sing

dancing *alizarin crimson*
swilling out layers of fear
resurfaced in anticipation

III

seascape

she surrendered to a rising crack
plunging in the oilwake of unnavigable *ultramarine blue*

tempestuous in *aureolin, burnt carmine* shallows . . .
thin ice escorted her demure course

IV

beware of undischarged colour

has she swallowed the vomit?
fresh grapes were pitied
undigested *florentine brown*
drawn under resentful *perylene scarlet*
showered on *naples yellow* lips
to entice   but whom

V

permanent english grey, how fair love was distraught
mars red laid on in the face of quivering shadows . . .
heavenly *monastral blue* half credible
how turbid – the bare madonna – covers her final irony

red iron oxide

I

in pleasure giving
scorched flesh-colour
is scraped back to *unbleached titanium*

on her ravaged body – adulterant silica
severed from its own grounds' shimmer
during sex has coalesced

II

no pigment simulates love's lies

ivory black bleeding solitary tints lay open

natural red iron oxide blunt reflections
interlocked with *venetian red*
counterattractions of fear

III

doggedly, seawards, *manganese black* turned about
from a hideaway caressing *mineral violet* buoys

nickel antimony titanium yellow rutty cement
iron blue ran out from under

IV

terra rosa on merry feet
'let fall'
deceptive *raw sienna*
scumbled in licentious *sepia* shadows
stepping out with *furnace black*
mock modernity in motion

V

pure cadmium vermilion red
love's rape

perinone red deep
indelible cobalt yellow wounds
bled in inadequate pigment

as it was lucretia's plight
to be replenished with such defiant cruelty

white lead

I

chromium oxide green
dissolved in tears

– stripped bare of her childhood's vows

pure cadmium zinc yellow
steeped in light and shade
over soiled dispatches of withering hues

urging the invisible

II

white lead / wild poppies
face to face with *manganese violet*
were transfixed

delicate *iodine scarlet* layers
mirrored in cold *fugitive red lake*
not having re-addressed the insult

III

nautical twilight: after William Turner

knuckled under, *silver white* whirls of the air
yellow ochre light deceptive forms
'full of twists and turns'
lay asleep

a *prussian blue* attrition . . .
ground into *wrought emerald* rays . . .
is blowing offshore . . .

IV

'fearless *black oxide of iron*' . . .
inexpressive undertones
under propellant infra-red, alas, matter

without embarrassment
the skipper's daughter is concealed
under an impassioned *azzurro della magna*

V

a hostile *vat orange* insoluble mass
unrelentingly partook of horror

intense *uranium yellow* rays shot forth
entwined with the limbs of destroyed children

gas black

I

geranium lake warped the berthing ground . . .
emerald green infinite linen laying out the anchor

selenium red shackles of dreams
voyaging in the prison of the eye

II

silent *gas black* immitigable thoughts
environed with *burnt sienna* storm-clouds
broaching to . . .

trotting *flake white*
fractiously drawn on charred waves . . .
etched with an unexpectant *nickel azo yellow*

ultramarine violet heightened . . .
perhaps it is that which bears the night in me

III

fair *brazilian wood lake*
hit on foreshortened trunks, shorn of shadows
yellow beeswax incised tears fused to *copper green*
melancholic acid
corrosively trickling down

IV

brutally anew, *antinomy yellow*
inked through its own savage spectrum

screened off
by *cadmium barium red* reflections

– declined with thanks –
indigenous to the landscapes of war

V

medusa's spectre
glaring *perylene maroon* reappeared

apart from *cadmium mercury lithopone red* dissembling
                                                brilliance
a new imitation unhinged *raw umber* 'insidious nuclear
                                                corpse'

reciprocally deranged, intermingled

love fragments

11 quintets

pleasure's sweet beginning has come to an end
– in the face of despair, whether
being in love or in blessed ignorance
notwithstanding flowers – and beauty withers
on all occasions, unmoved

quintet 1

I

self-partial
I wish of boredom a vow to tears

gnawed into melancholy . . . kissed at full lick
endeavouring to impose a surplus of waste

'gaily loved at a loss'

II

pleasure rejoicing in fear threatens

as a fetish magnificent to a child
ingrowing fantasies . . .
dawdling away under the jaw of secret bypaths . . .

being nailed down in me

III

boat-fly

>> each floating edge
>> hastened ashore

> hauled at a drowned heart
>> remediless seeking its amorous tedium
>> 'breakers ahead' into convulsions

IV

under the moon

unlike the saracen rally
its crescent split

ransacking apiece her concave youth

elsewhere delivered of a cowardly trophy
from below the desert

V

english ithaca

she, dearly self-begotten
weighed in with a compass set due-adverse

she, fully given over
point by sunken counterpoint to the insular cliff

    jumps for joy

quintet 2

I

callously fautless as a prizefighter
in the blended rounds of fuelled fisticuffs

beneath succulent strangers
he smote upwards the hooks in their disproportion

love itself counters

II

savagely torrid in their intercourse
having precipitated its heat

exuding a jealous vapour of love, brisk yellowish-grey
dissolved, off colour

III

merely a lover
self-sacrificed
st john the baptist
yields intemperance

granted for revelling in his beheading
        fair or foul in herself

          – she is sucking a waste of sperm

IV

as an autumnal child cedes its play
engrossed in exuberant nemesis

as in 'the dream of gerontius'
unfathomed centaurs
sprung 'bitter-sweet' from pernicious memories

V

she chose to adjust
cocky endearments towards languid syllables'
discrepant echoes . . .
risen in verse . . .
slurring lust an' love . . . without demur
in unviolated warmth

quintet 3

I

partaking of an injurious loss
could narcissus imperceptibly check

no matter, wilful odds on mirrors shown being laid . . .
       no matter, kissing by ever so much the staked
                    shadows . . .

II

       curbed of its cloistral bounds
       time forestalls by its leave

'a profuse sneer's distraught laughter'
       uninterruptedly self-contained in derision at
                   myself

III

how many hours' altercations' imaginary fears . . .
how much unmitigated nothing . . .
hastily surmised of change
how many over-lapping pawns are reversed

IV

boatpeople

unwieldily farther off . . .
the voyage surrenders its passengers

hand to hand a non-escape
resounding with floating illusions, eddying, drowned out

V

      whereas we tired of regressing
incestuously awake on watch . . .

love sets unbroken in deceit
      sheltered under a riot of joy – here where
            the night begins

quintet 4

I

for A.D.B.

on the sulphurous margin
waterlilies' sun-slaughtered blossoms
fell too dearly

with sleight-of-hand
eager to intercede for limpid shadows
    without tenderness

II

self-contradictory, mute st cecilia may befit
importunate nightingales

forcibly undertaken to proffer a cadence of love . . .
her own converted into fire
    music reeks aloud

III

instructed by her fathers how to propagate
            music and song

laying off a misused inheritance abroad . . .
voraciously seeming-silent . . .

such are the airs of athens

IV

drawn to luscious fountains
I submerged 'conjured out of jellied water'

no longer dictated by love in the guise of hatred
            (moreover indicative of a full-stop between
                                    ourselves)

V

time's hollowing out is seen in the flesh

chastened players with quarried toys
past counting their caresses
extracted their years
from the voice of guilt

quintet 5

I

tortuous hands
enforced on harrowing sheets to linger on . . .

engrained in morbid lustfulness
caressing the skin off stone

II

scant of fertility, worn away lilies
disintegrating as an old lover breathes strife

copious by default to recover youth's bursting grain . . .
nothing is abundant in me

III

revengeful on herself
       he himself is his own bridegroom
       ejaculating in a lurid sun

       mischievously pricking with its womanly spears
       the meadows of sensuality

IV

Richard Dadd
(oedipus coloneus)

in a blaze of sedulous violet crimson how fat boils
how it overclouds a lunar soul
embroiled with a million patricidal tears

(in a foreground congealed in dry rot)

albeit, am i a fire-watcher?

V

the night's image barters away its artificial wounds
inviting prostitution
befitting her scarlet lips at a brief price . . .

for a kiss – given to satiety – of the merest opulence

quintet 6

I

music seized by one thousand and one wrenched syllables
      devours her

           as one anguished pitch falling incessantly athwart . . .
             oozed out   perhaps in love

II

st john's fiancée

how   (a victim by default)
sumptuous salome is put to the test
cringing at the flavour of murder . . .
threatened with forbidding hunger . . .
absorbent of her desire to be embowelled aghast

III

redundancy – ipad

it meditates between cant and shadows

evident to a whiter space in its forged hermitage . . .
transverse sailing into the carcass of the night . . .

IV

isn't workandhelp, file-edit-view
so forcibly feeble a feat of arms?
hauled in hyper-pursuits . . .
            burrowed in dissoved images . . .
ephemeral-footed perforce

V

amateur boxing

as in want of defeat
the hook twists in a spate of frustration

hilariously bent, such a blow
aroused him to toil on further

in on it – again mopping up

quintet 7

I

letter-writing

disseminated fragments of love
unravelling a skein of life

each has broken off, shaken by either's intolerable content
       whimsically imprisoned in the mind

II

       no matter . . . a reflection on shadows
       slipped from the moon

narcissus endures

couched, self-complacent, in love with myself
no matter, losing footing
evoking unmirrored surfaces

III

entering into conversation

how many more hours mingled with fear
how much more futile inequity to rot

ill-fated, abruptly detached step by step
how many negligent seconds to pace

IV

the exit

surreptitiously the boatpeople were magnified
       dreamsagainstdreams submerged in conflict . . .
     having had to swoon with unruly pain and
                  a brutal vengeance . . .
   lying off . . .   outward-bound . . . from and on
                        to where?

V

simultaneously cast
at the wings of time
forearming its insolence
forged out of a timeless cheat
time's hollow shape knows how to reform

quintet 8

I

as a dionysian fool, music laughs loud and long

perverse towards melancholy
hers 'the shriek-beaten echoes of an unbending voice'
befallen to the harkening of silence
shatter too near . . . far off

II

nothing emergent yields itself to innocence

every bit as much hazardous
as sloughing off from the fissures of one's own flesh
the child-charmer

unbearably as it were shaken up

III

   what guarantees that time purrs 'oblivion'

irrespective of a chance intercourse
having dissolved the jelly of love in undevout
blunders, rest satisfied

IV

should I defer th'evening lisp
until retentive of memories
quarrying in the year one
one's disheartened utterance of flesh
cushioned too old in lassitude

V

as a satyr's flesh sloughs away
irresistibly striven to abet a rose made bitter-sweet

(a sinking flower too dreadful to break off
shedding love's aroma)

lust's whiff withers

quintet 9

I

jealousy

self-mutilated heavenly hands
slithering over a few strokes of genius . . .
fallen into narrow crevices

not without pity impressed onto their suffering

II

lovers ran foul
fertility's push has dried up

unwomanly blossoms further undertinted
belatedly drawn a blank

braced against the years of unavoidable wrath

III

boeotia

he, a freak of nature coaxed a still flight to hasten

>   back and forth unsexed vermilion air . . .
>   desultorily rising across on the bias

>   he in spite of himself paced out the ridge of
>   maturity

IV

the night's brawl quivers – on reflection

(in luminous range
he himself his estranged lover, no saturated steam
        covers the body of the transvestite)

V

unleashing 'tumult and scathing laughter'
at fair ophelia's dress

impinged on murderous nuances . . .

bouncing off umber into red
ancestral hues on which

delightful richard dadd had sworn insanity

quintet 10

I

dilated blossoms . . . sun riven . . . ebbing . . .
opened on the outer skin of innocence

sloughing off in my heart's mired shadows . . .
flowing inconsolable

II

perverse towards melancholy . . .
perhaps vying with deaf-mute nightingales
      hers 'the shriek-beaten echoes of an unyielding
                                  voice'
      befallen to the hearkening of silence
      shatter too near . . .
      far off

III

are we cancelled out . . .

self-reproachful
against a moist intercourse between ourselves
relinquishing heat . . .
tortuously having dissolved the ice of love
in its jellied sensuality . . .
            giddy with harassment

IV

should i defer th'evening lisp
until retentive of memories . . .
quarrying in the year one . . .
one's disheartened utterance of flesh
cushioned too old in lassitude . . .

V

as a satyr's flesh smoothes away
irresistibly lying to abet a rose made bitter-sweet

(a sinking flower too dreadful to break off
shedding love's savour)

            lust's whiff withers

quintet II

I

self-mutilated propelling hands
dismembered from caresses

stealthily impressed
in oarless massacres of sunken prints . . .
slithering on a few strokes of love . . .

      incised to rout
      steer no longer

II

woeful fertility's highs have dried up . . .

'blasted uneven
in amber primroses' boisterous prime
still wet
against wrinkled lovers'

precipitously being compared to dissipated blossoms
stirring

III

pythian

the morning's groom has buried the lagging sun
quenched under its bridal spears
botched up in placid drowsiness

steering through streamlets of dance

IV

the night's image is haggled over . . .
confluent mirrors are breaking down

reflecting on he himself his estranged lover
'no saturated steam'
covers the body of the transvestite

V

unleashing tumbled and skating laughter
at fair ophelia's soiled dress

perjured into a murderous dalliance . . .
bouncing off umber imitations of which
delightful richard dadd has lied

richard dadd

'The fairy's rendezvous'

septet

I

cleared of murder
richard dadd

from inherently unreconciled layers of colour
rapacious violet homicidal hues of patricide
roused up at the gambol of spiral jeers . . .
on a knife-edge, transverse shadowing, in delirium

with filial care

II

remember them
ah futility they said, farewell farewell
distress ever an' ever is their rest

an' yet an' yet

remember summers
remember fairies ah elves
nightingales behind downs
behind sunsets

death is fluttering its wings towards you

III

sworn by the rites of treason

life as told is dismal
the summer's short
winter clouds endure
roses an' violets not

anew misleading . . .
O on the forget-me-not
beauty is kept at bay
unshaken in flower

IV

Water Nymphs (etching 1841)

Afar in the proximity of Annabel Lee's azure darkness
    'beware of a haunting harmony'

many a plaintive anchored death
    weighing heavily ever after in the cause of dreaming

V

inclusive of richard dadd's 'A Father's Demur'
wantonyellowgreencrimson redeeming jests mishmash
of which he applied the odour of 'the fairy feller's
. . . master stroke' (immured in him)

VI

laugh if you will . . .

alternately flesh against flesh
withdrew

love, in peril of a striking mockery
weight of shadows
in gold an' silver

death on balance?

coral sunrises
vaulting ruby sunsets

were foreshortened . . .

VII

fairy dancing

discontinuously in full sway
'one knife was held in front the other behind'

skipping amok . . . an estranged partner sought cover in me
nothing else than 'among hyacinths I dream to die'

prosodion

I have flown to you
as a child to its mother
   (Sappho)

to my beloved teachers
Mr Kapetanakis & Nicolaos Plato

the dolphins of arion

rocked by the silent shifts
of night . . . one aqueous note
swooping upon
fourteen disruptive colours

minus five discordant sounds
pleading rebellion

the stringent third
redlunarviolet

in the voluptuous sixth
honed on music

hammers out the alluring bass

a dissembled love song

thus far in vain rebellion –
under poetic license to renounce
the beautiful irritant wasps

eager for the stings of poetry –
it was incumbent on you
swerving aside
to repel their throbbing invective

prosodion

> . . . all the day long they worshipped the god with music,
> singing the beautiful paean, these sons & daughters of
> the Achaeans, making music to the far-darter and his heart
> rejoiced to hear them
>   (Iliad)

Prosodion is an ancient Greek processional song in honour of a deity, mainly Apollo & Artemis. It was composed by poets or musicians of renown as well the various winners in festive competitions.

The orthodox east Byzantine processional liturgy as well as modern Greek secular music, evident in their ancient fountainhead i.e.song-form, reflect on time's unbroken progression.

The poem here sets out on a ritual march towards Modern Greece. Musicians, poets, dancers, places . . . are simply musical notes, steep steps ascending the rungs of time.

While having in mind a processional walk, Prosodion is compiled as a march of protest against the underperformance of divine Helen. No chronological order is followed. The whole of its parts, wilfully chosen at random, coalesce.

I'm coming: why d'ye shout at me?
   (Timotheus, lyric poet, son of Thersander)

music as played under the riot of silence

– is the past tense – abrogated
simulating a predictable future?

leto bride of zeus & mother of apollo & artemis
hermes' lyre . . . orpheus thamyris amphion . . .
the poet-priests anthes of anthedon pieris of pieria

arion of methymna . . . dionysian dithyrambs . . .
– set apart for the detours charting a course to ithaca

the pan-athenean festivals . . . light & shadow
iliad and odyssey . . . the women of homer

alkman – the maiden-songs . . . carian airs . . .
the sirens' voices . . . blocks of sound . . .
disrupted by dismembered ipiros . . . *ajax tassos xalkias*
                                        clarinet
ipiros macedonia rumely thrace shortened limb by limb . . .
disjunct hellespont . . . the pontic lyre its carnage . . .
wry asia minor   the singer panthea of smyrna in
                                        trepidation
sappho *moonlit home divine* . . . maenads with drums at
                                        cyprus . . .
manos loizou's 'sinuous tenderness'

. . . *aeolian crests of music rose 'n fell . . . blood-orange bleeding*

phoebus chrysanthus of the golden fleece music . . .

276

simultaneously cast . . . at the wings of time
forearming its insolence . . . forged out of a timeless cheer
time's hollow shape knows how to reform . . .

the homeric lyre . . . stavros kouyioumtzis gogos petridis . . .
born in bleeding fantak-olassa-trebizond

who art thou, O shipwrecked stranger
leontichus found thee here a corpse upon the
beach & covered thee in this tomb, with tears
for his own hazardous life; for no quiet life is his
either, but restless as the gull he roams the sea
    (Callimachus)

rugged euxine sea . . . listen to our prayers . . .

come sun, thou hurler of bright rays
at the everlasting skyey vault . . . send from thy bowstring
a far-flung shaft upon our enemies
O healer to whom we cry
    (Timotheus of Miletus – an exponent of new music)

st alexandros papadiamantis in conversation with the
                                 gorgons
euryale stheno medusa . . . mesomedes' hymn to nemesis

athenaus limenios' paeans . . .
erato the psalmist irene of tylos pyrrha wife of deukalion
kostas paskalis nikos zahariou . . . alexandra trianti agnes
                                   baltsa

the poetess telesilla's sweet tongue fed by bees
the dorian nightingale maria callas . . .
the parents and children of the family callias of athens
the choristers elpinikos and cleon at the games of 138 B.C.

the muse polymnia Aïs reaching on a convergent course . . .
nikos skalkottas dimitris mitropoulos iannis christou
iannis xenakis
. . . athenian school scene . . . aris garoufalis titos gouvelis
logothetis anestis michael adamis argyris kunadis demeter
terzakis
theodore antonio george apergis

manolis kalomiris face to face with panayiotis kokoras
dimitris sgouros leonidas zoras leonidas kavakos
winners at the sikyon music contest . . .
. . . kyknos 'the swan' legendary son of poseidon
the poet kostis palamas . . . enshrined in tenderness
ironlump words . . . manos anagnostakis titos patrikios . . .

blood on the ground (Euripides)
iannis ritsos . . . funeral procession . . . the mother's song . . .
a mere political verse . . . *electrons to electra . . .*
fugitive syllables . . . enduring consonants
embracing vowelless strings aimlessly singing . . .
spring-time worshippers . . .

monk auxentiou john chrysostom archbishop of
constantinople
melodious st romanos charioteer of pindar . . . nika's riot . . .
. . . *to what a beacon of light the ear listens . . .*

andrew of crete john of damascus cosmas of jerusalem . . .
theodore the studite . . . st isidore of seville
'the emperor' michael angelos terzakis . . .
the post-byzantine zeal of simon karas . . . lykourgos
angelopoulos
the singer-scholar domna samiou chronis aidonidis socrates
inopouloss
nectaria karantzi basil tsabropoulos spiros sakkas george
kouroupos
the seated minstrel eleni karaindrou

improvising heieieilisso . . . leeeeeee lelelelelele leeeee . . .
slave rhodopis mistress of the lesbian charaxus . . .
lingering menes . . . euripidean kourban
antony dalgas panagiotis kountas kostas vouros van
sofroniou
rita abadzi rosa eskenazi . . . kiki dimoula katerina
angelaki-rooke

manos hadjidakis fleur idantonaki mikis theodorakis
maria farantouri
dimos moutsis stavros xarchakos iannis markopoulos
maria dimitriadou thanos mikroutsikos melina kana
thanos papakonstantinou
manolis mitsias leonidas of tarentum vassilis lekkas
licymnius marios tokas *sleep laid the lad to rest with lids
wide open* . . .
eleni vitali eleftheria arvanitaki elli paspala haris alexiou
erotikos parios . . . honey sweet wine glykeria . . . ostas
makedonas . . .

thessaloniki – urban blues – grazed by 'mario'
konstantinou-stamatiou
'bees' by fotini velesiotou george skazantzis & helen
fotaki . . .
. . . full of twists & turns Greece secretes its melodies . . .

innermost rhythmical
'woman with round-based guitar' . . .

harmonia wife of cadmus of thebes
'epitaphs for animals' by anyte of tegea . . .
the rites of language . . . the euripidean forthcoming tears . . .
dionysios solomos andreas calvos konstantinos by kavafis

in the nocturnal choruses – shall I ever set my stepping
in bacchanising – to toss my throat into the dewy sky
like a frolicking fawn in the emerald joy of the meadow land . . .

the kitharode poets . . . arion of methymna . . . terpander's
choking fugue . . .
alkman ek m' elasas elgeon . . . you made me forget my
sufferings . . .
the initiator epigonus of sikyon akin to lasus of hermione . . .
. . . lysander of sikyon's whistling colours . . .
aristonicus of argos agelaus of tegea . . .
stratonicus of athens . . . tragedian sophocles nausicaa's
ball games . . .

the ridged fingers of sophocles papas dimitris papas aris
karastathis

alexandre lagoya evis sammoutis eva dimitris fampas
evangelos & liza assimakopoulos muse kleio antigoni goni
kostas grigoreas lakovos kolanian eleftheria kotzia . . .

no carcass of beef is here nor gold nor purple carpets
but a kindly spirit a sweet muse & delicious wine in boeotian cups
    (Bacchylides)

the pietà of el greco, music angled in tears
thales of gortyn archangel nikos xilouris alias orphic
                                 thaletas . . .

O treasure, lyre of golden haired Apollo
the light foot hears you and the brightness
your notes compel the singer when to lead out the dance . . .
the prelude is sounded on your trembling strings
    (Pindar)

. . . dispersed olive branches remnants of laurel leaves
clusters of ivy laid astray whirling round a vacuum . . .
aphrodite of knidos reputed as phryni-mnisaretis of boeotia . . .
the pamphylian poetess moira 'how estranged from you
                                     we are'

the bats . . . erinyes are nursing the night by stelios
                                kazantzidis . . .
(pleiads nymphs – the lovers maria polydouri kostas
                                karyotakis
while being pursued by orion were turned into doves –
                         then into stars)

further progression . . . besotten poets and musicians . . .
katarina gogou nikolas asimos paul sideropoulos . . .
markos alexiou george trantalithis george filippithis . . .
evi siamanta free jazz semela mother of dionysos . . .
sakis papadimitriou floros florithis savina iannatou stephan
                                                  andreathis . . .
mimis plessas dimitris kalantzis . . .

kick the rock & out the birds will fly
    (Aristophanes)

parched violet flowing echoes . . .
kefalos ithaka corcyra lefkas paxos zakynthos kythera . . .
anacreon ibycus theognis' opulent drinking cups . . .
the public sex performers dionysus eleuthereus
the tanagran housewife corinna
the love of mimnermus for elegiac aulete nanno
purple rejoicings . . . the erotic odes
xenocrites of locri . . .

the songs of epagathus . . . the choir-aulis
hypsipyle . . . deidameia . . . androgynos
hector's ransom . . . medea . . . antiope

. . . idly barking marcus vamvakaris magical notes . . .
orphic-reared st romanos the melodist . . .
nun eikasia the wardress of languid sins . . .
mari kaninou's elusive temper reverberating
against vasilis tsitsanis' apollonian outbreak . . .
meleager's *up, fly, yes fly O musician O gnat*

gregory bithikotsis demetra galani . . .
romani michael angelopoulos
theophanes nicias simmias swooned for joy . . .
callimachus the alexandrian . . . amorous iannis

papaioannou

    . . . *'the fair is forever dear'*
      (Euripides)

  . . . fragmentary landscapes:
the shrine by the gulf of aenos holds the words:

'in which future tense will the language of memory
retaliate?' as in 'I will requite for its abandon'

pursuing satyrs' sacrificial march after cerberus . . .
nereid kallipoli peninsula bemoans a (distressed)
callitelis . . . twice-raped thamyris lover of hyacinth . . .

overlaying the roofing of poseidon's
temple with the skulls of defeated strangers to antaeus . . .

precursor alexandra fostered by the poet lycophron . . .

troades re-emerging . . . kassandra's maddening climax
aeschylus persae 'tear at your breast too'
thalattathalatta 'theseathesea' . . . ebbing from trebizond . . .
the river lethe a loss of memory allotted to the fountain-

head

of byzance . . . detritus in constantinople
the hiss of genocides . . . the rape of virgin mary

the akathistus hymn's alternate rejoice . . .
the child myrtle never bearing malice

life filtered through the pores of impassioned melodies –
with its elusive manifest changing key

pelops husband of hippodamia founder of the olympian
$\qquad\qquad\qquad\qquad\qquad\qquad\qquad$ games . . .
$\quad$ . . . the restive satyr antonis foniadakis O graceful one

rapturous bodies muscle-bound ceased to dance
indulgently infirm deliciously unremitting . . .
swerving tortuously under bloodshot performers
chartered to the lydian mode . . .

timotheus' erotic cheer . . . a ritual-song-dance . . .
$\quad$ . . . *for ye must foot it wide-paced lads & dance your revels better*

the priest antipater of thessalonika . . .
heavenly anyte of tegea telesilla erinna fair myro praxilla
$\qquad\qquad\qquad\qquad\qquad\qquad\qquad$ of sikyon
corinna . . . she who sang of the dreadful shield minerva
$\qquad\qquad\qquad\qquad\qquad\qquad\qquad$ bore
myrtis of anthedon sweet nossis . . . eftihia
$\qquad\qquad\qquad\qquad\qquad\qquad$ papagianopoulou . . .
cyrene *la fille de joie* vibrating in modern greece
O dearest of women . . . sotiria bellou . . . i pray for you

beastly-drunken dionysus . . .
grates on the undulating boundaries of music . . .

the dolphins of arion quivering throbbing stringed . . .
anchored to love's rhythmic waves (apollo's dispersal
accelerating from fair alkman to the compass-amplitude
of the seagull Aïs – I.X.)

if beauty grows old, share it before it be gone
and if it abides why fear to give away what thou dost keep
    (Strato)

the muse thalia's abodes

'formerly the dead left their city living –
but we living hold the city's funeral'
(anon)

Delos sanctuary of Apollo and Artemis. Epidauros theatre
                                                built by
Polykleitos the younger. The Odeon of Herodes Atticus.
                                            The theatre
of Dionysos. The theatres of Zea, Oropos, Aigina, Delphi-
                                                    Phokis,
Evia-Eretria, Oiniades, Stratos. Dodona, Omolion,
                                        Demetras, Corinth,
Elis, Sikyon. Koulmos' cavity – partial auditorium.
                                            Thion-Pieria,
Vergina, Philippi, Maroneia-Rhodope, Melos, Delos,
                                        Kos. Metapontum,
Ephesus, Pergamon, Halicarnassus, Troy. And so forth . . .

The actor of the city of Ikarios in Attica begs his leave.
'i sing nothing that had not its witness'
(Callimachus: fragment)

Brief Biography

ILIASSA SEQUIN was born in 1940 on a small island in the Cyclades, where her father was a high school teacher. Soon after the family moved to Athens, living under the Acropolis in Plaka. Writing poetry from an early age, Iliassa initially enrolled in the Panteion University to read social and political studies. Against her father's wishes she changed course and enrolled in Carolos Koon's theatre (with her stunning looks an acting career loomed).

With musicality in language uppermost in her concerns she developed an original poetic style expressing a severe disquiet for the status quo. This led to her being befriended by Odysseas Elytis (later a Nobel prize winner). He saved her from an attempted suicide when her father forbade her attending the theatre – even going as far as threatening to sue the theatre for allowing Iliassa to attend without paying fees. In 1958, abandoning her studies, she ran away to Germany. From then on she flitted between Germany, Italy, France and Sweden (the playwright' Peter Weiss and critic Susan Sontag offering accomodation and moral support), only returning to Greece for the briefest of visits.

Fluent in all these languages, existing frugally on temporary jobs throughout the 1960s, she met and corresponded with many poets including Giuseppe Ungaretti, Paul Celan (who became a close friend), Louise Kaschnitz and André du Bouchet. Very recently, Iliassa translated his poetic commentary on the painter Bram van Velde, *Le Couleur*, which remains unpublished.

In later years, English being her second language – she would insist it was her first – she saw her poems published in *L'Ephemère*, *L'Ire de Vents* and *Les Belles Lettres* – in English with French translations. In London, through the sculptor Brian Wall, she met her husband-to-be Ken Sequin (at that time a reportage illustrator) and commenced writing plays for a puppet theatre (she tried to have her highly political plays performed, without much success).

Through the painter/writer Trevor Winkfield publishing some of her poems in his magazine *Juilliard*, Iliassa came to the attention of John Ashbery, who published her in the *Partisan Review* – leading her to become associated with the New York school of poetry.

Moving to Yorkshire in the mid-1970s (Ken taking a lecturing post there) Iliassa continued her quintets, often delving into the terminology of off-beat cultural norms alongside notions of romantic pastoral life. Then, on a visit from his adopted home in New York City, Trevor Winkfield accompanied the pair on a visit further north to Scotland. There he introduced Iliassa to Ian Hamilton Finlay who, intrigued by her non-confessional, formally innovative style, suggested that Ken and Iliassa should not dawdle too long in Yorkshire. This, together with Ken's deteriorating health (Iliassa insisting that this was due to the stultifying lifestyle of academia imposed on art lecturers), prompted their return to London in 1992.

With Ken painting again, Iliassa embarked on new work; as always exploring the musicality of language. Themes such as the sinking of the Kursk submarine in the Baltic (G.M. Hopkins' poem *The Wreck of the*

Deutschland being an inspiration), the plight of the refugees arriving in Greece being another, poems flew from her antiquated iBook. She translated the aforementioned poem for André du Bouchet and saw some of her poems appear in France – notably in *La Treizième* edited by the poet Max de Carvalho. A selection of her correspondence with du Bouchet is also being prepared for publication.

Otherwise little has been published – apart from in the New York journal *Conjunctions*, which published some of her many quintets. *Cinema Sextet* – inspired by the work of Ken Loach and Richard Dadd (an exploration of the Victorian painter's psyche) also came out bilingually in *La Treizième*. Her work also appeared in the *Exact Change Yearbook*, New York, 1995, and in *The Sienese Shredder*, issue 3, 2009. Iliassa had only one chapbook published in her lifetime: *quintet*, published by Peter Gizzi in *o-blék Editions*.

Notes and Acknowledgements

Quintets 1–5

o-blék editions, 1991
ISBN: 1-879645-03-3

Versions of these poems have appeared in *Un Poco Loco* and *o-blék*.

Utility Chapbook # 2
The Garlic Press
P.O. Box 1242
Stockbridge, Massachusetts 01262

This Utility Chapbook entitled *quintets* was designed and typeset by Peter Gizzi for o-blék editions. 300 copies were printed in Providence, RI; Spring 1991. 26 copies are lettered and signed by the author.

Words on poetry

First published in the French poetry journal *La Treizième* in 2001, translated by André du Bouchet.
   In 2007 the English text with André's letters to Iliassa was also published in *La Treizième*.

Kursk

The Russian nuclear-powered Oscar-class submarine *Kursk* sank on 12 August 2000 in the Barents Sea, during a naval exercise. All 18 personel on board were killed.

Iliassa worked on this series on and off for over a decade. Hopkins' poem *The Wreck of the Deutschland* was its catalyst.

Richard Dadd

In 2016 Iliassa garnered together from her collections a selection titled *richard dadd*. An edition of (hand-made) books – fewer than 20 – was dispersed among friends.

Acknowledgments

Thanks goes to Nancy Anderson for her invaluable skills typing up manuscripts and to Melina Doumy for checking spelling in 'Prosodion' and elsewhere.